Quod scriptura, non iubet vetat

The Latin translates, "What is not commanded in scripture, is forbidden:'

On the Cover: Baptists rejoice to hold in common with other evangelicals the main principles of the orthodox Christian faith. However, there are points of difference and these differences are significant. In fact, because these differences arise out of God's revealed will, they are of vital importance. Hence, the barriers of separation between Baptists and others can hardly be considered a trifling matter. To suppose that Baptists are kept apart solely by their views on Baptism or the Lord's Supper is a regrettable misunderstanding. Baptists hold views which distinguish them from Catholics, Congregationalists, Episcopalians, Lutherans, Methodists, Pentecostals, and Presbyterians, and the differences are so great as not only to justify, but to demand, the separate denominational existence of Baptists. Some people think Baptists ought not teach and emphasize their differences but as E.J. Forrester stated in 1893, "Any denomination that has views which justify its separate existence, is bound to promulgate those views. If those views are of sufficient importance to justify a separate existence, they are important enough to create a duty for their promulgation ... the very same reasons which justify the separate existence of any denomination make it the duty of that denomination to teach the distinctive doctrines upon which its separate existence rests." If Baptists have a right to a separate denominational life, it is their duty to propagate their distinctive principles, without which their separate life cannot be justified or maintained.

Many among today's professing Baptists have an agenda to revise the Baptist distinctives and redefine what it means to be a Baptist. Others don't understand why it even matters. The books being reproduced in the *Baptist Distinctives Series* are republished in order that Baptists from the past may state, explain and defend the primary Baptist distinctives as they understood them. It is hoped that this Series will provide a more thorough historical perspective on what it means to be distinctively Baptist.

The Lord Jesus Christ asked, *"And why call ye me, Lord, Lord, and do not the things which I say?"* (Luke 6:46). The immediate context surrounding this question explains what it means to be a true disciple of Christ. Addressing the same issue, Christ's question is meant to show that a confession of discipleship to the Lord Jesus Christ is inconsistent and untrue if it is not accompanied with a corresponding submission to His authoritative commands. Christ's question teaches us that a true recognition of His authority as Lord inevitably includes a submission to the authority of His Word. Hence, with this question Christ has made it forever impossible to separate His authority as King from the authority of His Word. These two principles—the authority of Christ as King and the authority of His Word—are the two most fundamental Baptist distinctives. The first gives rise to the second and out of these two all the other Baptist distinctives emanate. As F.M. Iams wrote in 1894, "Loyalty to Christ as King, manifesting itself in a constant and unswerving obedience to His will as revealed in His written Word, is the real source of all the Baptist distinctives:' In the search for the *primary* Baptist distinctive many have settled on the Lordship of Christ as the most basic distinctive. Strangely, in doing this, some have attempted to separate Christ's Lordship from the authority of Scripture, as if you could embrace Christ's authority without submitting to what He commanded. However, while Christ's Lordship and Kingly authority can be isolated and considered essentially for discussion's sake, we see from Christ's own words in Luke 6:46 that His Lordship is really inseparable from His Word and, with regard to real Christian discipleship, there can be no practical submission to the one without a practical submission to the other.

In the symbol above the Kingly Crown and the Open Bible represent the inseparable truths of Christ's Kingly and Biblical authority. The Crown and Bible graphics are supplemented by three Bible verses (Ecclesiastes 8:4, Matthew 28:18-20, and Luke 6:46) that reiterate and reinforce the inextricable connection between the authority of Christ as King and the authority of His Word. The truths symbolized by these components are further emphasized by the Latin quotation - *quod scriptura, non iubet vetat*— *i.e.,* "What is not commanded in scripture, is forbidden:' This Latin quote has been considered historically as a summary statement of the regulative principle of Scripture. Together these various symbolic components converge to exhibit the two most foundational Baptist Distinctives out of which all the other Baptist Distinctives arise. Consequently, we have chosen this composite symbol as a logo to represent the primary truths set forth in the *Baptist Distinctives Series*.

REASONS FOR SEPARATING

FROM THE

GENERAL
SYNOD OF ULSTER

ALEXANDER CARSON, LL. D.
1776-1844

REASONS FOR SEPARATING

FROM THE

GENERAL SYNOD OF ULSTER

BY

ALEXANDER CARSON, LL.D.,

MINISTER OF THE GOSPEL

With a Biographical Sketch of the Author by John Franklin Jones

Edinburgh: J. Ritchie
1807

he Baptist Standard Bearer, Inc.
NUMBER ONE IRON OAKS DRIVE • PARIS, ARKANSAS 72855

Thou hast given a *standard* to them that fear thee;
that it may be displayed because of the truth.
– *Psalm 60:4*

Reprinted 2006

by

THE BAPTIST STANDARD BEARER, INC.
No. 1 Iron Oaks Drive
Paris, Arkansas 72855
(479) 963-3831

THE WALDENSIAN EMBLEM
lux lucet in tenebris
"The Light Shineth in the Darkness"

ISBN# 1579788432

CONTENTS.

	PAGE
Preface	xi

CHAP.
- I.—Reasons *a priori*, why it is probable that the Scriptures contain a Divine Model of Church Government 1
- II.—If there be a Model of Church Government in the New Testament, what is the Nature of that Form we are warranted to expect? . 9
- III.—On the Obligation of Apostolical Practice . . 21
- IV.—Presbytery Examined 29
- V.—Of the Office of Lay Elders 39
- VI.—Of Independency 50
- VII.—The Independency of the Apostolical Churches proved from the Apostolical Injunctions, and inferred from other circumstances in the Epistles 65
- VIII.—Objections Answered 72
- IX.—Reasons why some are apt to conclude, that there is no Church Model in Scripture . 80
- X.—Character of Church Members—or the necessity of Pure Communion 87
- XI.—Objections Answered 96
- XII.—Additional reasons for Separating from the General Synod 105
- XIII.—Objections Answered 119

PREFACE.

Every Christian is a member of two kingdoms perfectly distinct, but perfectly compatible in their interests. In each of these he has peculiar duties, in the discharge of which he is to pursue a very different conduct. As a subject of civil government, he is called to unreserved, unequivocal obedience, without waiting to inquire into its nature and quality, or even the legitimacy of the title of those in power. If he understands his Bible, he knows that "the powers that be, are ordained of God," and that he must "submit to every ordinance of man, not merely for wrath, but also for conscience sake." In Britain he will submit to monarchy; in America to a republic; and in France he will obey, without puzzling himself in determining whether Buonaparte be a legal governor, or a usurper. But it is not so in the kingdom of Christ. Here it is his duty in everything to judge for himself, and in no instance to be the disciple of man. He is commanded to examine, not blindly adopt the dogmas of his spiritual guides. He is nowhere required to conform and submit to that form of church government, under which he has been educated, or to which he may at any time have thought it his duty to attach himself. He is enjoined to "prove all things, and to hold fast *only* that which is good." He is

Christ's freedman, and should not suffer himself to become the servant of man, nor to be fettered by human systems.

Convinced that this is both the duty and privilege of every Christian, I have largely and leisurely examined the *original nature*, and *present state* of that church* in which I was educated, and in which I have for some years acted as a minister. I have examined, and am convinced, that both in *plan* and *administration*, it is contrary to the Word of God. It must appear to every man of candour, that I could have no interest in deciding as I have done. Every interest of a worldly nature was surely on the other side. The day I gave up my connection with the General Synod, I gave up all that the world esteems. I sacrificed not only my prospects in life, and my respectability in the world but every settled way of support. It is usual for men to desert a church under persecution; I have deserted one in the tide of her prosperity, or as some of her friends speak, in her "*meridian glory*." If people never begin to think anything amiss in their religion till they are persecuted for it, or till superior honours and advantages are held out to view, they have reason to suspect their judgments. But when wealth and respectability in society are in the gift of the church, when one of her members sits in judgment upon her, she is likely to get a fair trial. A man is not apt, upon slight grounds, to reason himself out of his living,

---

* I am obliged sometimes in this pamphlet to use the word church in this common acceptation, though not so used in any part of the New Testament.

his friends, and his reputation. It will not be out of whim he will exchange ease for labour, respect for calumny, present competency for the naked promise of God. Notwithstanding this, I am perfectly aware that the worst motives and designs will be attributed to me. I would indeed know little of human nature, and less of the Bible, if I did not expect the reproaches of the world. If they have called the Master of the house Beelzebub, much more those of his household. He himself experienced such treatment from the world, and he knows how to succour his children in like circumstances.

The divine right of the Presbyterian form of church government, it may be expected, will now become the *present truth* among all sects of Presbyterians in this country. Their inveterate rage against each other, will for a time be suspended, that they may unite against the common enemy. Every pulpit will resound with the cry of innovation; many an affecting representation will be given of the sufferings of our worthy forefathers, in erecting the *venerable fabric.* I would caution Christians not to suffer themselves to be imposed on by such senseless declamations. The appeal on both sides must be to the Scriptures; not a stone of the fabric can be lawfully rested on other ground. If classical Presbytery be in the New Testament, let its advocates come forward, and fairly refute my arguments. I have no object but truth, and whatever may be published against my pamphlet, in a Christian and candid manner, shall receive every attention. But let them not lose their temper, nor substitute railing for argument. Neither let them nibble round the surface of the subject, but let them enter into the essence of the debate. If any are convinced, let them beware of stifling convictions. Let them not suffer interest, prejudice, or the fear of reproach, to deter them from obeying *the least* of the commandments of Christ. "Whosoever shall be ashamed of me and my words in this sinful and adulterous generation, of him also shall the Son of man be ashamed when he cometh in the glory of his Father with the holy angels."—Mark viii. 38. "He that loveth father or mother more than me, is not worthy of me; and he that loveth son or daughter more than me, is not worthy of me. And he that taketh not his cross, and followeth after me, is not worthy of me. He that findeth his life shall lose it, and he that loseth his life for my sake, shall find it."—Matt. x. 37–39.

Though I am decidedly convinced of the complete independency of the apostolical churches, and of the duty of following them, I would not be understood as placing undue importance upon this point. Christians of every denomination I love, and I will never, I hope, withhold my hand, or my countenance from any who, after impartial investigation, conscientiously differ from me. I can from my heart say, " grace be with all those who love our Lord Jesus Christ, in sincerity and truth." Pity indeed, while there are so few friends of Jesus, that those should harbour hard thoughts of each other, for conscientious differences. But let it not be expected from this, that I shall " know any man according to the flesh," or avoid freely censuring whatever I judge unfounded in Scripture, out of compliment to any friend who may countenance it. This would be to " walk as men."

In endeavouring to overthrow the system of Presbyterianism, I have only assaulted the main pillars of the edifice; if I have succeeded, the roof and all the rubbish will fall of course. The voluminous defences of Presbytery, of former days, I consider too stale to be particularly noticed. I wait till their advocates recognise them. But though every pin of that system could be proved to be divine, it would not affect my opinion of the duty of separating from the Synod. I would stand upon ground still tenable. I do not shrink from discussion. Truth will finally prevail.

CHAPTER I.

REASONS A PRIORI* WHY IT IS PROBABLE THAT THE SCRIPTURES CONTAIN A DIVINE MODEL OF CHURCH GOVERNMENT.

NOTHING can be more unfair than to determine *a priori*, with an air of demonstrative certainty, what must be revealed in Scripture; and then to open the book and compel it to favour the hypothesis. We are not arrogantly to prescribe to God what he must reveal; our conclusions upon what is proper to be revealed, must be ultimately determined by a candid inspection of the sacred volume itself. Controvertists upon the subject of church government have frequently abused this argument; and have, as it were, almost settled the dispute without opening the Bible. Their favourite system must be *there*, and they are determined to find it. In proportion to the poverty of Scripture materials, is there a wider scope for imagination; where Scripture fails them, *high probability* will amply compensate for the deficiency, and is even more convenient, as it will vary according to the necessities of the different writers.

But though this argument has been abused, we are not on that account entirely to abandon it. I apprehend that there is a legitimate use which it may have on many questions, highly serviceable, if restrained within its natural limits. Though we are not warranted to conclude with certainty, that there is a divine model of church government in the New Testament,

---

* By *a priori*, I mean those arguments that render it probable, that there is in the New Testament a Divine Model of Church Government, previous to the investigation of Scripture, and I use it here and elsewhere to prevent a circumlocution.

till we prove it from itself, yet there may be reasons
to render the affirmative extremely probable; which,
when considered, will animate us in our search, induce
us to collect the scattered fragments, and prepare us
to receive, with gratitude, even the scanty pattern
which Scripture may afford. Suppose I live near a
river on which there are many bleach-greens—after a
flood I find a web—I am anxious to know to whom it
belongs, for many have been lost. I instantly conclude
that it will tell its owner itself—I open it, and examine
the ends for the owner's name, but to my great surprise, though both are entire, I find no name. I recur
to my argument *a priori*—I reason thus: Can it be
possible that a linen-draper would be so careless as not
to mark his cloth? This web is entire—therefore
certainly it must have a mark, though I cannot discern
it. Encouraged by this, I unfold the web, and glance
hastily over it from end to end; but no mark can I
find. Shall I give over? No: The principle upon
which my expectation is founded, remains unshaken,
therefore it must be owing to my unskilfulness that I
am unsuccessful. I am not accustomed to the business,
and therefore the mark has eluded me. I begin again—
I search more leisurely; not a thread of the woof
escapes my eye. As I advance I see some little strokes
marked thus (\11)—this cannot, I say, be the mark;
however I will keep it in view. I proceed again, and
in a little I find some other of the same unintelligible
specks (HH). Strange! what does this mean? These
are not letters, say I, yet they are not accidental. I
advance in hopes of some clearer discovery, but all I
can obtain is something like the rest (ΛII). The
thought occurs to me to bring these together, and try
what they will make when joined. At last, after trying
and fitting them a thousand ways I make A H. Over-
joyed, I exclaim, this is Mr. H—'s, my neighbour's
web. Just so I reason, and so I act upon the subject
under consideration. I see an evident necessity for
Scriptural direction on this head. I perceive strong
antecedent reasons to expect that the New Testament
will contain the model of the apostolical churches for
our direction. With these sentiments I open the Bible;

I read and read, collect and compare, and when I get the scattered fragments to make an harmonious whole, I am not doubtful of its divine origin.

1. Human manners are much affected by the difference of civil government. The genius of the constitution gives a turn to general manners and modes of thinking. Nations have their characteristic habits and customs which the philosopher can trace to this source. May not the same effects be expected from particular forms of church government? This influence may not be discernible in a comparison of two individual Christians, trained under different forms of church government, but will be sensible when sects are compared in the bulk. The government that is most spiritual will unavoidably communicate a tincture of its spirit to the mass of its subjects. Now, if the mode of the government of the church be in the smallest degree influential of manners, I cannot conceive that Christ would leave this to human discretion.

2. The different theories which have been adopted on this subject, have materially influenced the sentiments of their respective advocates, not only in the explanation of the passages of Scripture immediately concerned, but also of many in which they are not under the influence of a party spirit. All Scripture truths have a mutual connection, and it will often inevitably happen, that adopting a wrong theory upon one point, will lead us into other mistakes in the interpretation of Scripture, or hide from us the true key of analysis. To those who have attentively studied this controversy, it will appear evident that the elucidation of many places in Scripture is affected by it. Now, if a difference of opinion on this subject affect the explanation of other passages in Scripture, there is, besides its own importance, an additional reason why it is worthy the interposition of God.

3. The general sense of professing Christians in all ages, argues the necessity of Scriptural direction on this point. This argument is used with success in favour of revelation, and I see no reason why it should not have all its weight here. The great bulk of professing Christians have in all ages supposed, that they

have found in Scripture, at least the ground-work of their respective plans. When was the *divine right* given up? Not till the enlightened advocates of worldly churches saw that it could no longer be pleaded with advantage. When they found that the witness would not speak in their favour they endeavoured to keep him out of *court*, lest he should speak against them.

4. Either unanimity on this point is not a duty, or the Scriptures must afford us the means of effecting it. Now, the apostle frequently calls our attention to this as a duty in all things. True, indeed, perfect unanimity is not to be expected, but is this the fault of a defective revelation, or of our remaining corruptions and blindness. There can be nothing a duty which is not revealed. Our differences in the greatest *minutiæ* of religion are owing to ourselves, and not to a want of Scripture direction. Now I know of no way to effect unanimity, but by proposing self-evident truths, or the authority of God in revelation. That the mode of church government does not belong to the former, is sufficiently evident from experience; it must therefore belong to the latter. But unanimity upon this point is *consequentially* of more importance, than upon many others of more *intrinsic* importance. Upon many other points, if Christians have differences of opinion, they have it to themselves; upon this their difference affects each other. Either I must submit to be ruled by the opinion of my neighbour, by a church government which I think Christ did not appoint, or he must do so to me, or we must form different sects. Now upon many other questions perhaps more intrinsically important, each of us may hold our own opinions, and bear with each other in the same church. I cannot think then that God would leave us without Scriptural direction on this matter.

5. Will there ever be a day when all sects shall coalesce? I can see no reason to doubt of this. Without it, I cannot conceive that perfect harmony the Scriptures, with the general consent of professing Christians, give us reason to expect. Discrepancy on this point is too great to be consistent with the *increase*

of knowledge of the latter days. Whether is this to be effected by a new revelation, or by a more plentiful effusion of the Spirit upon Christians, and a greater attention to the *revealed will* of God? Is there any other way in which revelation can effect this union, but by giving us a model, or directions on this point? I think it not supposable, that the want of a model in Scripture would be a means of uniting all Christians. For if there be no model or direction in Scripture, unanimity or uniformity is not a duty. This would be saying, that the opinion that union is not a duty, would effect union. Never would there be a greater variety than when this notion should prevail. To effect union, on this supposition, it would appear to me to be necessary to enlarge the powers of the human mind, beyond what hath ever yet appeared in man. The sublimest geniuses on earth have their differences of opinion on every thing but self evident truths. But to effect union in this manner is derogatory both to revelation and the office of the Holy Spirit.

6. There cannot be that prompt, cheerful, and dutiful obedience to church rulers, if the model and laws of the church be not in Scripture. If church rulers have a discretionary power to enact laws, they may abuse that power, and therefore their decrees must be received with examination and caution. Thus there may be a difference of opinion with regard to their propriety; and, at all events, the conviction of the duty of obedience will be more slowly and circuitously obtained. This will gradually introduce either a spirit of disobedience, or of abject servility, among church members. They will be led either to slight the authority of church judicatories, or receive their dictates with a slavish submission. The truth of this remark is abundantly evidenced among those sects which more or less claim the right of acting according to circumstances; of enacting *laws of expediency and discretion.* The people are either the slaves and dupes of their church rulers, receiving the decrees of ecclesiastical assemblies, as the dictates of heaven; or they make light of, and despise their authority. Complete, unequivocal, cheerful, and conscientious obedience is to be found only

among those who dare not command without opening their commission, and appealing to the laws to which they enforce obedience. Here there is no room either for disobedience on the one hand, or slavish obedience on the other. Church members see clearly they are not obeying man but God.

7. Either all forms of church government are alike calculated to promote edification, or if one be better than another, that which is best will be so evident, that all Christians will readily agree in it, or the Scriptures must afford us sufficient means to discover it; otherwise they are deficient. I know not that there are any who will agree to the first, and it appears from fact that the second is not just. In the same times, in the same city, we find almost all the varieties of church government that have existed in times and countries the most remote. Now, if it be a matter of importance to adopt one form rather than another, and if the children of the same family, as well as the inhabitants of the same city, will differ in their opinions on this subject, it would appear to be a matter worthy of divine interference. If there be no divine model, I cannot see how God is not to blame for all the variety of sects occasioned by difference of sentiment on this subject. If we are left to our own judgment and prudence, there can be no sin in using them; and a variety of sects is the unavoidable consequence.

8. Whatever is left to human discretion in religion, is of such a nature that there is no room for the weakest Christian to err, nor the least foundation to dispute; nor would the smallest advantage have accrued to the church, by having those things determined, which are left undefined; but on the contrary such a determination would have been attended with inconveniencies. Such, for instance, are the times of meeting for public worship on the Lord's day, the order of the services, &c. Who ever complained that these things were not confined? Would it have been of any advantage to Christians, that Christ had appointed certain stated hours for public worship? Nay, would not this have been attended with many inconveniencies? But it is quite otherwise with the point in question. The deter-

mination of this would have been attended with no inconveniencies, but with many and important advantages. The leaving of it undetermined would give unavoidable occasion to dissention and schism.

9. Civil government and legislation require the highest exertion of human genius, and the greatest men who have written on the subject, are by no means agreed even in theory, what is the form best calculated to promote the happiness of mankind. In what respect is church government a less important or difficult matter than civil government? nay, I conceive the former to be the more difficult, by how much the government of the mind is more difficult than that of the body, and the more important as spiritual is greater than temporal happiness. Is it then supposable that Jesus would leave a matter of such importance to the discretion of man? Besides, Christ's disciples, upon whom this duty would devolve, are the unfittest imaginable for such a business. They are generally "the weak things of this world." True indeed, they all have spiritual wisdom, for "they are all taught of God;" but this requires political rather than spiritual wisdom. It is evident that every *human* form of church polity is, and must be, on the model of the most approved civil polities. A Christian then to be calculated for a legislator in the church must have the qualifications of a civil legislator. But the great body of Christians are destitute of these pre-requisites. They must then either yield to be led implicitly by the few learned and enlightened men among them, or be liable to the greatest mistakes.

10. I suppose there is not another question in religion about which so much human blood has been shed, or on account of which the earth has been filled with so much confusion, as this very question. Does not this argue the necessity of a divine model, that God may be vindicated, and the blame be wholly attachable to man?

11. If no divine model be given, it would have been impossible to prevent ambitious men from imposing on the simplicity of the multitude, and promoting schemes for their own aggrandizement, under the specious cover

of zeal for religion. Such men as Diotrephes would always assume the pre-eminence. Antichrist would on this supposition have some apology. Nay, in such a case some sort of Antichrist is unavoidable; and it is not very material whether he be one man, or several hundreds. I do think, then, that to leave the Christians of the first ages without excuse—that men may be clearly chargeable with the guilt of rearing and nurturing that monster, it was necessary that a divine model should have been given, from which the smallest deviation was sinful.

CHAPTER II.

IF THERE BE A MODE OF CHURCH GOVERNMENT IN THE NEW TESTAMENT, WHAT IS THE NATURE OF THAT FORM WE ARE WARRANTED TO EXPECT?

1. THAT form of church government which is practicable in all countries, ages and circumstances, is likelier to be the Scripture model than one which is not. Now there is no country, age, or circumstance, in which the Independent plan is not practicable; but to make either Presbytery or Prelacy practicable, there must be a number of congregations formed in a particular district. If there were but a single congregation in a kingdom, the Independent government would not be affected; if every individual of a nation were a Christian, it is equally adequate. In the former situation Presbytery could not exist; in the latter, if there were a sufficient number of pastors for every congregation, a general assembly would be altogether unwieldy. Independency is not fitter for one country than another; Presbytery and Prelacy are each peculiarly suited to one form of civil government rather than any other. The former was suited to the Republic of Geneva, the latter to the Roman Monarchy. Independency meddles not with the state, but in things civil, conscientiously obeys " the powers that be," *whatever be their form or quality.*

2. That form of church government that is capable of the least abuse, is the likeliest to be divine. Now unquestionably this is Independency. If a particular church on this plan degenerates, becomes erroneous, or indifferent, it has no power to injure others, or draw them into its errors. If all the Independent churches of a nation were to degenerate except one, that one cannot be compelled or overawed into their errors.

But it is quite contrary with Presbytery. When one congregation becomes dead or erroneous, it has an influence on all the rest; and when such become the more numerous, they have power to corrupt those that are more pure. On the other hand, in a period of general lukewarmness or apostacy, if any particular Independent church be impressed with the duty of reformation, there is nothing in their connection with other churches to clog or prevent them: but a congregation in such a situation among Presbyterians would find the whole weight of the connection hanging upon them, and that it would be absolutely impossible for them to succeed, without bringing the majority of the whole body to their mind, or by separation. I know indeed it is said, that Presbytery is better calculated to prevent error from creeping into congregations, by the power the majority claims over the minority. But how should one man, or one congregation, keep another from error? By compulsion or persuasion? I apprehend there is no lawful means for one church to keep another from error, but by remonstrance and exhortation. Nay, there is no other method, can be successful: if this fails, pains, penalties, imprisonments, confiscations, and death would be useless. Force may make hypocrites, but will never make a Christian. A law of synod may prevent a minister from preaching error, as to the five points, but can it enable him to preach "the truth as it is in Jesus?" Will it enable "the blind to lead the blind, without both falling into the ditch?" Where is the great difference between poisoning the sheep, and starving them? But let the history of synods vouch their utility and efficacy in restraining error, and preserving vital religion. They may, for a time, preserve orthodox, in *the letter*, but midnight darkness may reign with an orthodox creed. "The natural man cannot know the things of the Spirit, because they are spiritually discerned." Vital religion seems in a great measure extinguished, even among those sects who make the highest pretensions to orthodoxy. A violent wrathful spirit of party, and an ardent zeal for human forms and human creeds, seem pretty generally substituted for spirituality, and catholic

Christian love. Now, all the means of remonstrance, persuasion, exhortation, and entreaty are equally open to Independent churches, to preserve each other from backsliding and error. An Independent church may reform other churches, but can receive no injury from them: a Presbyterian congregation may be injured by its connection, if they are corrupt, but cannot reform them in any other way than what is practicable by an Independent church. I conclude then, that as Independency hath all the advantages without any of the disadvantages of Presbytery, as to their influence of connection, it is more likely to be the Scripture plan.

3. It is a maxim in philosophy as well as in divinity, that God does nothing in vain. According to this, if all the ends of government can be obtained in an Independent church, all foreign interference being useless, cannot be appointed of God. That a church under this form of government can subsist in vigour, is evident from experience; and that it is capable of exerting all necessary influence in preserving others from backsliding, we have also seen. What possible advantage can be gained by a numerous subordination of courts? If a light hat of fur be sufficient to preserve my head from the weather, why will I cover it with a mill-stone?

4. That form of church government which cannot preserve purity of doctrine without human expedients, is not so likely to be the Scripture model, as that which can attain and preserve the highest possible degree of vital religion, as well as purity of doctrine, without admitting, in any instance, the devices of the wisdom of man. Now it is generally acknowledged by Presbyterians themselves, that it is impossible to preserve uniformity of opinion among them, without a Formula or Confession,* of Faith, to be publicly recognized by

---

* The utility and lawfulness of human confessions and creeds, as standards of religion, does not lie immediately in my way at present, but as Christians in this country seem very generally in this instance "to be carnal" and walk as men "teaching and receiving for doctrines the commandments of men," I earnestly recommend to their serious perusal a late pamphlet by Mr. Ballantine of Elgin, entitled "Observations on Confessions of Faith

their members. Now, it must be evident to every unprejudiced person, that there is no formula in the Scriptures. That constitution, then, that requires one to maintain purity, is not likely to be of God. The same may be argued from the necessity they are under, to decide by majorities instead of unanimity; debarances, invitations, tokens of admission to the Lord's table, &c.

5. That form of church government that leads us most to the Scriptures, and requires in church-members the greatest acquaintance with them, is the most likely to be that of the New Testament. Now, without an intimate acquaintance with the Bible, Independents cannot advance a step in church affairs. I might speak from what I have witnessed of the knowledge of the Scriptures among Independents. I speak only of its necessity, arising from the constitution of their churches! With them it is absolutely necessary not only in church rulers, but private members. The Bible is their code of laws; they have no other confession or book of discipline. They can do nothing without it; it must be continually in their hand. The rulers rule only by the Word of God. But a man may be a Presbyterian all his life, either pastor or private member, with a very slender acquaintance with the Bible. The knowledge of forms and of ancient usuages, of ecclesiastical canons, and books of discipline, are the chief qualifications that are necessary for a Presbyterian judicatory.

6. That form of church government that needs most the presence of God and prayer, is the most likely to be the divine model. Now the Independent is the only plan in which there is, strictly speaking, room for the *manifest* interposition of God. There are instances in which prayer is their only resource. Their doing all things by unanimity, creates a peculiar necessity for prayer. If there be but one member of a different mind from the rest, it is the same as if there were the one half. In such a situation, the promised

of Human Composition," &c. Their attachment to these is the greater, as they have not been accustomed to hear their authority questioned by any, but those who are enemies to the doctrines which they contain.

presence of Jesus is their only refuge; prayer is their only remedy; and when the difficulty is thus removed, which perhaps will scarcely ever fail, if explanation, remonstrance, and intreaty be affectionately applied, all the praise will be seen to belong to God. On the other hand, a Presbyterian court can proceed as independent of God as a court of civil justice. True, indeed, it is usual to ask him to preside; but can they not proceed smoothly enough without him? Is there ever a situation in which they are not as competent to do business, and settle the most critical affair, as the Parliament of England? I cannot think, then, that an institution is of God's appointment, which does not *need* God's presence.

7. That form of church government which is most favourable to liberty of conscience, in which the individual experiences the least undue influence in determining his principles and conduct in religious matters, is the most likely to be the Scripture model. The Scriptures are the only rule of faith and practice, and every man is bound to judge of them, and determine their meaning for himself. He may use helps to understand them; but if he understands them differently from others, he is bound to act upon his own belief, rather than that of another. Now this liberty can be completely enjoyed as a right in no other than an Independent church. True, indeed, in some Presbyterian connections, individuals may enjoy all the liberty they desire; but does this flow from the nature of the constitution of classical Presbytery, or from the indulgence, or indifference of those connected with them? The very leading idea in Presbytery, that for which it is most prized by its greatest admirers, is this very power of restraining principle and conduct in matters of religion. If Presbytery is robbed of this power, what end does it serve? It is then nothing more than a selection of members from different congregations met for counsel and advice. But where is the Presbytery that acts solely upon this principle? If there be any, they are, as to constitution, Independents. There are indeed Presbyterian connections, in which individuals may be Socinians or Calvanists, but this is the result

of connivance in the general body, and not the genuine fruit of Presbytery. Whenever the body chooses to claim its right, a majority may compel an individual to embrace every shibboleth of their creed, and direct and circumscribe his labours as they please. But view genuine Presbytery among the stricter sects, and it will clearly appear that in all things there must be a complete uniformity. Forbearance is not known. I do not say that we are bound to hold religious intercourse with any individual, or body of men, that we judge destitute of the truth. But as long as we can look upon a man as a brother *born again* and walking in the commandments of God, we are bound to exercise forbearance towards him in other matters of comparatively less importance. But if there are some Presbyterian connections liberal as to principle, are they equally so as to religious conduct? Can any of their members enjoy the privilege of acting for himself, as well as of thinking? Is he not amenable to their bar, if he transgress any laws of theirs, although he judge them contrary to the laws of Christ? I conclude, then, that although from connivance, there may be more liberty of conscience in some Presbyterian connections than others, yet as a power of compulsion is inherent in the very nature of Presbytery, it is not likely to be the Scripture model.

8. Nothing is more universally felt in the human heart than ambition. Nothing our Lord found more difficult to repress in his immediate followers. That form of church government, then, which affords the fewest incitements to ambition, is likely to be the model which he would pitch upon. Here also, the Independent will stand foremost. It is not capable of an adulterous alliance with the world. Its spiritual nature has no charms to tempt the meritricious embraces of worldly men. Though Presbytery is not the most exceptionable in this view, yet it is not without objections. It has been courted by, and wedded to the world, and a hideous progeny has issued from the connection. It has fought for, and in its turn obtained temporal power and riches; and whilst it held the sword, it was more like to Mahomet of Mecca, than

Jesus of Nazareth. The forensic nature of their courts, also, is too much calculated to foster pride, by inducing men to aspire to be the leaders of parties, and make a figure in assemblies, collected from every part of a province or kingdom.

9. If there be any particular model of church government in the New Testament, it is probable that the enlightened advocates of it will rest the cause on the same foundation, however various may be their arguments. For if several intelligent men embrace the same model, and have the same means of information, they have every inducement to unanimity, and if uninterested, or unprejudiced, are likely to defend it on the same general ground. If they take different and opposite hypothesis to serve as a ground-work for their superstructure, they are not likely to have had a common ground in Scripture. Now the advocates of Presbytery take quite different grounds to rest it on. Some defend the whole machine as divine, to the smallest pin. Others pretend to see only the skeleton in Scripture, with a power to fill up the outlines. Others defend it as a lawful human system, upon the grouud that we are bound to no particular mode of church government in Scripture. Some find the Presbyterian elder in Scripture, and some make him only a prudential human expedient. Some give him a seat in ecclesiastical assemblies in his own right; others in right of the people whom he represents. They are as divided also about the right of nomination of elders. Some give this right to the congregation, or seat-holders, whether servants of Christ or of Satan; others claim it for the old session. Now, I think the inference which any rational, disinterested, unprejudiced man would draw from this, is, that they have no common source from which they draw their ideas. If they had, certainly Presbytery would not be such a camelion. If they all saw the same picture in the Scriptures, surely they would not give so many contradictory accounts of it, when it was their interest to agree. If Presbytery had been in Scripture, of all its friends Dr. Campbell of Aberdeen, was the best able to defend it; yet Dr. Campbell gives up its divine right, and proves beyond

contradiction, that the apostolical churches were Independent. If ever Presbytery could be found in Scripture, the luminous and penetrating mind of Dr. Campbell, who lived and died at the head of a Scotch university, would certainly have traced it.

10. The end of church government, and church meetings of every kind, must be the edification and growth of the members, and the promotion of brotherly love. That form which is best calculated to promote these ends, is the most likely to have been instituted by Christ. Now, we might rest this upon matters of fact, in favour of the Independents; but we shall content ourselves by observing, that their peculiar advancement in experimental religion, deadness to the world, devotedness to Christ, zeal for His cause, and love towards the brethren, are much the result of the principles of their constitution, in which they are distinguished from other societies. Some of these are their separation from the world, into a spiritual communion, in which they can all look upon each other as Christians, upon good evidence—their frequent church meetings, and mutual public exhortations—the care and watchfulness that every member has over every other as his "brother's keeper," and not committing church power to a few—the opportunity of discovering every talent, and occupying even the smallest in its proper sphere—the close union of all the members rich and poor, each acting on the other as the different wheels of a watch set in motion by the main-spring. Their church order resembles the Macedonian phalanx, which so long as it kept its ranks, was invincible. There is here no possibility of playing the coward; each encourages, and in a manner compels the other to do his duty, as a good soldier of Christ. When individuals are under temptation to give ground, and begin to backslide, the whole body acts as a rere-rank, to encourage them to behave valiantly, to support them when overpowered, to give them an opportunity to rally when they are thrown into confusion, to prevent them from running from the field of battle, and to push them on again to the engagement. The great piety and zeal discovered in individuals of other sects, is no

objection to this. Such persons would have been still more eminent, had they enjoyed a purer communion. There may be healthy men in a very unhealthy climate. This, however, would not induce any man to say, that India is as healthful a climate as Ireland. Compare the nature of the church constitutions, and then compare the general body of the members of the one, with that of the other, and if you are unprejudiced, you will not be long in suspense. I forbear to draw a picture of the generality of Presbyterian connections: it is really too hideous to be reviewed. Besides, many of the evils among some of them, are not the necessary result of the Presbyterian constitution.

11. Christ's institutions father themselves. If a child had been lost, and after many years, several pretenders had come to the father, and there be not sufficient evidence from testimony to determine between them, would it not be very proper to look for a resemblance to the parents, and their other children, either in bodily appearance, temper, or genius? If such a striking resemblance is found in any of them, it will be instantly concluded that he *fathers himself.* In the same manner it is reasonable to expect a family likeness in all the ordinances and works of God. Let us then apply this rule in ascertaining the divine legitimacy of the form of church government. Christ has had such a child, but he has been exchanged at the nurse, and a vile impostor has been imposed upon the world, during all the dark ages of the reign of Antichrist. Since the reformation, various pretenders have laid claim to the honour of heavenly birth. It might be highly serviceable, in judging of their pretensions, to compare the features, mien, temper, and genius of each claimant, with those of the father and his other undoubted children. I shall content myself at present, by examining and tracing a few of the lineaments of two of them, Presbytery and Independency.

God's wisdom is foolishness to the world, and the wisdom of the world is foolishness with God. Whatever, then, be the divine form of church government, it is evident that it must not be one which would be suggested by human prudence or policy, that it may appear to be of God, analogous to his procedure in other instances, and having a necessity for his presence and guidance. It must be one which would appear defective and inadequate, in the estimation of the wisdom of this world, that God may have all the glory of upholding it himself. This is exactly the manner of the divine procedure in every other instance. The wisdom of the world expected Christ to have appeared in far different and opposite circumstances, and to have acted in a quite contrary manner, in erecting and establishing his kingdom; but the divine wisdom appears in this, that the almighty power of God is manifested in accomplishing what had evidently no other support. As the Gospel was first propagated by means the most unlikely to succeed, in themselves the most inadequate; to show that the unseen hand of God upheld and spread it, and that the divine procedure be consistent, it seems necessary that the government be seen solely to rest on *Immanuel's* shoulders. As this King was introduced and inaugurated, and his kingdom erected in a manner directly the reverse of human prudence and policy, so also is it probable will he govern it. To conduct the government of his kingdom upon any of the plans of human governments, by measures and assemblies formed upon a worldly model, would be inconsistent with the whole conduct and procedure of Jesus.

Now, if there be any justice in this reasoning, a very child may apply it to the point in hand—nay, let our enemies themselves be the judges. The very arguments by which they support Presbytery, the very objections which they make to Independency, fully prove to which of them this character belongs. Presbytery has every feature of a child of this world's wisdom. It is entirely a political institution, every part of it analogous to civil polity. In this view, it is really a vigorous republic, and so far as its power extends, it shows that it knows well how to exert it. Its decision, by majorities, instead of unanimity; representation in ecclesiastical assemblies; subordination of courts; and the right of appeal; forms and etiquette of business, &c., are all borrowed from the world. On the contrary, Independency, like Christ himself, has never approved itself to the wisdom of this world. Nay, the only arguments that can plausibly be urged against it, is its insufficiency for any other than *primitive times*. In no civil institution in the world, are the distinguishing features of Independency to be found. It could not govern a private family of unregenerate men. It has been called by those who did not understand its constitution, the *purest democracy*, but it is evident that it is rather a *Christocracy*. Christ alone governs. There is not a law or regulation left to the wisdom of man. What civil government ever existed, in which the unanimous consent of every member was necessary, in every instance ? Human affairs could never be conducted in this manner, nor could a body of unconverted men be governed in a church in this way. Nothing but the unseen, almighty power of God could have protected and propagated the Gospel, in the circumstances of its appearance, opposed by all worldly powers ; nothing but the presence and power of Jesus could make the simple machine of Independent church government, effect its end. I conclude, then, that if a likeness to God, and an analogy to his procedure in other instances, be any token of childship, Independency, and not Presbytery, is the lawful heir.

But let us pursue the comparison in some other instances, and we will see that Presbytery has not a feature of the family. In all the institutions of God there is a remarkable simplicity, but classical Presbytery is the most clumsy and complicated machine that could possibly be invented, and a tedious round-about way of settling differences, and transacting church business. Several hundred men, from the most distant parts of a province or kingdom, meeting annually, besides all their subordinate meetings, is a thing that bears no resemblance to the simplicity of other Gospel institutions. When united to those, it is like a sober, plain-dressed gentleman, with a huge military hat and feather; or like a small neat chapel with a towering steeple. But peep for a minute into their general synod or assembly. What pomp, what stateliness, what importance do they assume! See yon young orator artfully apologising for his youth, and this aged gentleman looking importance from his years of standing. Stop a little; here is rudeness; "*chair!*" "*chair!*" there will be a quarrel about a trifle; "but the apostles quarrelled at Jerusalem." Here now are several days spent, and what is done? Nothing about religion for its advantage; nothing but what could have been done to better purpose in any congregation.

I might trace the picture much further, but I shall only barely mention, that Presbytery is too expensive for a "kingdom not of this world." The other children of the family live on a trifle; if this is the heir, he is a rake.

CHAPTER III.

ON THE OBLIGATION OF APOSTOLICAL PRACTICE.

HAVING given some reasons to show the antecedent probability of a divine model of church government, with some observations with respect to the plan we are entitled to expect, before I proceed to examine the Scriptures respecting the claims of Presbytery and Independency, I shall endeavour, in this chapter, to establish the obligation of the practice of the apostolic churches. Not that this is more necessary to me than to the true Presbyterians, but because it is beginning to be fashionable with the members of worldly churches, when they are driven from the Scriptures, to take refuge in *the liberty of deviating from the example of the apostles.**

1. The combined weight of all the arguments *a priori*, fall into the scale of the obligation of the example of the apostolical churches. We cannot positively determine what the Bible contains, till we examine it; but if there be every reason antecedently to expect a divine form of church government, and if it is possible to trace the practice of the apostolical churches, is there not every reason to look upon this as the divine model, exhibited in the Scriptures as an universal pattern? The arguments *a priori*, I grant are inconclusive, if no form could be pointed out from the Scripture; but if it be possible to ascertain the constitution of the apostolical churches, I see no good

---

* Dr. Stillingfleet is the great patron of this hypothesis. In his *Irenicum* he endeavours to unite Presbyterians and Episcopalians, by proposing a scheme of a sort of Presbyterian-Episcopacy. But to effect this, it was necessary for him to rid himself of the obligation of taking the apostles of Jesus Christ for an example. I originally intended to have followed the Doctor through his performance, but I found I could not do so without exceeding all bounds.

reason why they should not have their full force. Like an 0 in figures, they draw all their value from their situation; standing alone they are worth nothing; united to the approved apostolical practice, I do not see how their worth can be depreciated or their force invalidated. If a divine plan of church government be extremely necessary, by what authority does any man reject the apostolical?

2. Not only the general sense of professing Christians is on the side of the obligation of apostolical example, but the very advocates of the contrary opinion evidently betray their chagrin, that it is not in their favour. How anxious are they to catch at every thing that looks like approving of their respective churches? What abundant pains do they take to detect every part of the system of their adversaries, that is not apostolical? Every sect goes as far as it can in company with the apostles; it is not till they cannot follow, that the apostles are acknowledged as insufficient guides. Did ever any man think of this hypothesis, till he found apostolical practice against him? Could any of the worldly churches produce uniform apostolical practice on their side, how would they triumph?

3. If the apostolical churches are not a model to us, then all those numerous Scriptures that are employed in describing them, or in giving them directions, are useless to us. Why is such lumber contained in the Word of God? All Scripture is said to be "given by inspiration," and "to be necessary;" but if we are not to imitate the apostolical churches, there are many passages in the New Testament that are now absolutely useless. Accordingly, it is very evident how uninteresting such portions of Scripture are to all that hold themselves at liberty to deviate from apostolical practice. Such persons have a much more barren and jejune revelation than others.

4. Either the apostles acted by divine direction, or by their own wisdom, in the constitution of churches. If the latter, they would undoubtedly have told us so, as they do in less important matters. But even on this supposition, I think the judgment of an apostle is entitled to more respect than to be rejected without the

most urgent necessity. I would really prefer the private opinion of Paul upon a matter of expediency, to that of a whole general council. But if, as there is every reason to believe, they acted by divine command, the form of church government they instituted, can never be changed but by the same authority. If any form is better than another, surely the apostolical is the best. It cannot then be a matter of indifference whether we follow the best, or adopt a worse. If the Holy Ghost had judged it expedient to adopt a different form in a different period, or in different circumstances, would we not have some intimation of it? Without a divine license we are not at liberty to alter or infringe in the smallest degree. We may as well assume the right of altering any other apostolical institution as that of church government.

5. There can be no danger in the closest imitation of the apostolical churches. Is any man sure that he does not displease God by refusing to imitate them? Between the certainty of pleasing, on the one side, and the possibility of offending on the other, the choice which a Christian should make, is evident.

6. No person who pleads the authority of apostolical example for the first day Sabbath, or any other purpose, can consistently reject it in this instance.

7. A plan in model and not in systematic description, is what we are entitled to expect. A direct and formal treatise on the subject, which some people look for, would be altogether anomalous in Scripture. After-ages are no where addressed but in the person, as it were, of the apostolical churches: we are not known but as members of them. Whatever is said to them, is said to us. Thus our Lord, promising his continual presence with his servants in preaching the Gospel, addresses them all in every age, in the person of the apostles then present, " Lo, I am with *you* always *to the end of the world.*" " Where two or three of *you* are met, there am I." The apostles also speaking of what was to happen in every after-age, address those to whom they write as concerned, and warn them of what was to happen to us and our successors to the end of the world. " We, which are alive and remain unto the coming of

the Lord, shall not prevent them which are asleep." Here the apostle addresses, in the person of the Church of the Thessalonians, which then was, those Christians which shall be on the earth at the time of the second coming of our Lord. I might quote innumerable examples, were it necessary. Now this being the case, that after-ages are addressed only in the person of apostolical churches, how absurd is it to expect a formal treatise on church government? Every necessary instruction must have been given in the forming of the churches. How preposterous would it be for an apostle, after he had formed a church, and left it, to write a treatise to that church, on the method of forming a church! All then that can be expected, is an incidental account of apostolical practice. The subject cannot be formally, but indirectly, and, as it were, unintentionally handled. Suppose, for instance, the apostle Paul had founded the churches of Edinburgh, and after his departure, had written a letter to them, to establish them in the faith; would any rational man expect a treatise on the constitution of a church, which he had already constituted? No, all we could expect, would be an allusion to what he had done. I say, then, according to the analogy of the manner of revelation, there is not room for any other information on church government, than an account of apostolical practice. Here, I think, Dr. Campbell fails of his usual acumen, or he would not have expected the subject treated in "another manner," upon the supposition, that we are absolutely bound to the constitution of apostolical churches. But some other observations on this subject, I will reserve to another place.

8. The tabernacle itself, was made according to model, and not from a verbal delineation, or treatise. "Moses was admonished of God, when he was about to make the tabernacle. For see (saith he), that thou make all things according to the *pattern* showed to thee in the Mount." Now we have also a pattern in the Mount, for our New Testament churches are exhibited to us in those of apostolical constitution. To this pattern, we are to look for every part of our constitution and discipline. Let every man take care that he make everything in a Gospel church, after the pattern of that exhibited to us in the

Scriptures. This is a divine model; to add to it, or take from it, will spoil the beauty, and diminish the strength of the building.

9. We are often called upon, to be followers of the apostles, without any exception or limitation. By what authority then do any except from this rule, the conduct of the apostles, in the formation of churches? From every general command, I think there can be no lawful exception, but what is impossible, sinful, or otherwise determined. If we are called upon without reserve, to follow the apostles, I think the injunction extends, not merely to their conduct as men, but particularly as our examples in all church affairs. If I justify a quarrelsome disposition, from the example of Paul and Barnabas, I am condemned by the Scriptures. But this quarrel was not recorded for nothing. It is for an example, to guard us against such a temper. If any one would contend for the duty of celibacy, from the example of Paul, his example, in this, is declared not to be binding. If any man would take it into his head to work miracles, like the apostles, this is impossible, without receiving the power of an apostle. Yet these, and such as these, are the mighty objections, alledged by Dr. Stillingfleet, against the obligation of apostolical example. But I ask, is the imitation of apostolical churches sinful, impossible, or otherwise determined, in any part of Scripture. If not, I demand a reason for excepting it from the general injunction.* With what reason, then, does Dr. Stillingfleet refuse, with triumph, to be bound by apostolical example, till we produce him an express command, for that particular instance? May we not, with the same reason, demand a positive

---

* Not only the conduct of the apostles in the churches, is exhibited as an example to us, but their very antecedent characters, as well as their after-trials, supports, joys, &c., are recorded for our encouragement, instruction, or example, to avoid or practice. The great design of the Almighty, in allowing the rebellion of Paul to proceed to such a height, is said, to be an example to us, that the most notorious sinners might not be afraid to come to Christ.—1 Tim. i. 16. Paul's declining to avail himself of his right to live by the Gospel, and his working with his own hands, are declared to be for an example to Christians to support themselves by industry.—2 Thess. iii. 9.

command, at the end of every apostolical example? Here is a general command; let it be shown, why this particular instance of the obligation of their example, in the constitution of apostolical churches, should be excepted. Besides, if the observation above be just, that we are known only as members of the apostolical churches, what room was there for a command to after-ages, as distinct from that in which they wrote? An express command to a church, to continue the form of government, which an apostle instituted, we would think superfluous. This is always supposed, without a positive declaration to the contrary. No, it lies not upon us to produce such a command, but on those who take upon them, to set aside the obligation of apostolical example; it is certainly incumbent, that they should produce their warrant. If God instituted the Independent plan, before any man can warrantably deviate from it, it behoves him to produce from Scripture a specific license.

10. But though the manner of divine revelation forbids us to expect a direct address to after-ages, upon the obligation of apostolical practice, yet we have what is equal to it. There are instances in which an older, completely organised apostolical church, is exhibited as a pattern to others, more imperfect. Now, if the apostolical churches are exhibited as a model to others, and if some are praised or blamed for their conformity to, or disagreement from them, it is very clear, that the apostles intended that all churches, in every age, should be upon the same model. 1 Thess. ii. 14—" For ye, brethren, became followers of the churches of God, which in Judea are in Christ Jesus." 1 Cor. vii. 17— " And so ordain I in all churches." 1 Cor. xiv. 33— " For God is not the author of confusion, but of peace, as in all churches of the saints." Here, the same order is intimated to exist in all churches. But how is God the God of order and peace in all the churches of saints, if he has not ordered every thing himself? If he has left men to choose their form of church government, and to make laws for themselves, could it be said, that he is not a God of confusion? The confusion that would exist on that supposition, would be bound-

less and endless. 1 Cor. xi. 16—" We have no such custom, neither the churches of God." Here, the other apostolical churches are exhibited, as a model to this. 1 Cor. xvi. 1—" Now, concerning the collection for the saints, as I have given order to the churches of Galatia, even so do ye." Here, the example of the churches of Galatia, is exhibited as a model to the Church of Corinth. Titus i. 5—" For this purpose, left I thee in Crete, that thou shouldest set in order the things that are wanting, and ordain elders in every city, *as I had appointed thee.*" Here, we see, that in setting in order the things that were wanting, even the evangelist Titus, was not left to his discretion, but was to act in every thing, *as Paul had appointed.* Titus had his instructions, as an officer from his general. Can we pretend to greater power?

11. Is it possible for a church to exist and flourish without observing any other laws, rules, or regulations, without any other offices, or modification of offices; without any other discipline, or sanction of discipline; without any other test of admission, or means of preserving purity; but what are to be collected from apostolical example, and the scattered information of Scripture? If this question can be answered in the affirmative, what apology can men plead for their innovations? The advocates for a liberty of deviating from the form of apostolical churches, lay the weight of their cause upon this argument : " No form of church government, could answer all ages, countries, and circumstances." What do men mean by this jargon? Do they mean, that no form would answer for a civil establishment, under every form of civil government? Do they mean, that none could be given to suit the various humours of carnal men? Yes, the true meaning of this objection, if they would put it into words, is, that no one form could be given to serve as a part of a political system, under different forms of civil government—that the simple apostolical model, suited only apostolical times, being incapable of governing that mixed multitude, of which all worldly churches consist—and that it was unsuitable to the dignity of an aspiring clergy. But these are the very credentials of its divine appointment. It

is eminently calculated to govern Christ's children, who, like the Spartan youth, have their minds moulded to their laws; but it will always be found to fail, when members are admitted, not of the character of the members of apostolical churches. Nay, one impure member, if not cut off, when detected, would stop the harmonious procedure of the whole machine, as effectually as a watch is stopped by the accidental admission of a hair. But, can a man be pleased with the prostitution of his wife? Can Christ be pleased, or his cause advanced, by the prostitution of his ordinances? Shall the spiritual kingdom of Christ, change its appearance, with the fluctuating opinions of the world; the varying laws of temporal kingdoms; or the caprices of carnal men?

CHAPTER IV.

PRESBYTERY EXAMINED.

HAVING, in the preceding chapters, stated some reasons to render a divine model of church government probable—having shown some characteristics of that which is likely to be the Scripture model—and endeavoured to establish the obligation of apostolical example—let us now proceed to inquire *what is actually the mind of the Scriptures upon this point?* Let Presbytery first come under review. One thing I would premise, as a caution to myself and all who treat this subject—*Let us never forget, when we are interpreting Scripture texts, that they are the words of the Holy Ghost.* He that forces them, to make them countenance, or avoid discountenancing his system, is guilty of an attempt to compel the Holy Ghost to speak a lie, and bear false witness. How guilty! how infamous is the wretch that employs, or compels another to perjure himself to serve his interest! But how much more criminal and infamous is the man who would put a forced interpretation on the language of the *Holy One!* I have heard a man say, that indeed it was very criminal to employ a person to *swear a lie;* but if at an assizes he should run short of an evidence, he would think no great harm of getting one *to swear the truth for him*, though he was not a witness of the truth of the matter. I am afraid there are too many Scripture critics who act upon this principle. They lay it down as a matter indisputable, that such a tenet is true, and expressed clearly in some passages of Scripture, and therefore they will set about to silence, or force other texts to compliance, by perversion. Let us then attend simply to the testimony of plain Scripture, in its plain acceptation. It is really the interest of the Christian, if he could allow himself to think so, to discover and embrace truth, though it should deprive him of the dearest earthly possession.

Another thing that must be attended to, by all who plead for the divine right of any particular form of church government, is, that nothing be admitted but what is clearly founded in the Scriptures, either in precept or example. Those that pretend a divine model, must produce it, without the help of conjecture, or probabilities, to complete it.

The great bulwark of Presbytery, according to its friends, is contained in the 15th chap. of the Acts of the Apostles. Let us therefore examine this portion of Scripture, by the rules of candid criticism, and see if in any thing, it gives its countenance to this mode of church government.* The matter of fact related, seems to be this: certain teachers had gone down to Antioch from Judea, who had inculcated the necessity of the observance of the Mosaic law. From verse 24, it appears, that if they were not actually sent out by the Church of Jerusalem, to preach the Gospel, they at least wished to have it understood, that they had apostolical authority. The Church of Jerusalem, in their letter, acknowledge that they went out from them; and do not deny their being sent by them; but affirm that they had no such doctrine in charge from them, as the circumcision of Gentile converts. Previous to this, Paul and Barnabas had returned thither from their first itinerancy. Of consequence, they opposed this doctrine; and after they had much fruitless discussion upon the subject, it was resolved by the brethren in Antioch, to send Paul and Barnabas, and certain others, to consult the apostles and Church of Jerusalem, from whom these teachers had come out. But let us read the chapter with calmness and attention, and we will see that it contains not one feature of modern Presbytery.

1. Where do we find here the Presbyterian subordination of courts? Was the matter first tried by the church session at Antioch? Was it next carried to a Presbytery?

---

* This subject is fully and ably discussed by Mr. Ewing of Glasgow, in "A Lecture on part of the 15th chapter of the Acts of the Apostles," which the reader would do well to consult.

Was this appeal from a Presbytery at Antioch? Who sent Paul and Barnabas to Jerusalem? It will puzzle the most metaphysical head to discover a session and a Presbytery, or either, at Antioch; yet, if it cannot be proved that this appeal came from a Presbytery of ministers and lay elders, at Antioch, the meeting at Jerusalem cannot be a synod.

2. If this be allowed to be a synod, it will cut off all superior and inferior courts. There cannot be a superior court, for this determined for the whole Christian world, and from it there could be no appeal. There cannot be subordinate Presbyteries and church sessions; for this appeal was not from any inferior court, but immediately from the brethren at Antioch. I know it is said, that the Presbytery of Antioch deputed Paul and Barnabas; but it is easier to say this than to prove it. The antecedent to the verb "determined," is not clearly expressed. The structure of the sentence, if the sense of the passage would admit, would allow Paul and Barnabas, or the false teachers themselves, or both together, to be the persons, who, "determined." But this will make nothing for Presbytery; nay, it would overthrow it. For if Paul and Barnabas, or these with the false teachers, or if the latter only, "determined" to depute the messengers, there is an end to Presbytery. It is no unusual thing, however, in reading the New Testament, to be obliged to look back a little for the antecedent to the verb, or to take it from the general sense of the passage. The most natural interpretation is, that the brethren deputed Paul and Barnabas; or that it was done conjointly by the brethren, the false teachers, and Paul and Barnabas. This is clearer, from the words, as they stand in the original, which are more literally translated: "They *appointed* Paul and Barnabas, and certain other of them, to *go up*," &c. The false teachers could not appoint Paul and Barnabas to go up to Jerusalem, nor is it likely they desired it, as they must have known that they received no such *charge* from that church. But, be this as it will, upon no supposition could they have been sent by a Presbytery, because no such thing is mentioned in the connection. Whatever be the antecedent to εταξαν,

it must be found among the persons spoken of in the preceding verses. It may as well be said that the magistrates of Antioch sent them, as the supposed Presbytery of that place. There is the same evidence for the one as the other. Besides, if the appeal had been from a Presbytery, would not the answer have been to the appellants? The letter of the Church of Jerusalem would not have been addressed to the brethren, which are of the Gentiles, but to the Presbytery of Antioch?

3. This assembly carried all things by complete unanimity; therefore can be no model to any assembly, in which a majority decides for the whole. Suppose it to have actually been a synod, no decree of a modern synod could plead its authority, which was not carried unanimously.

4. Suppose this to have been a synod, it only warrants their meeting, as a matter of dispute may arise among the churches. It would give no countenance to regular periodical meetings. But Presbyterian courts have their stated meetings, whether or not there be business of importance to justify their meeting.

5. The decision of the Church at Jerusalem was obligatory, not only in the Church of Antioch, which had appealed, but upon all churches in the world. In the letter, verse 23, Syria and Cilicia are expressly included. And in Paul's second journey, he and his companion gave the churches, in the cities through which they passed, the decrees ordained by the apostles and elders at Jerusalem. Will any man say, that there were representatives from these places, in the Jerusalem assembly? It cannot then be a model for a synod, where none are bound, but those represented. If synods will quote this for a precedent, they must no longer confine themselves, to make laws for their own connection, but decide in matters of religion, for the whole Christian world. But, as this assembly consisted solely of the members of one church, if it be a warrant for foreign interference of any kind, it will prove, that an individual church, consisting of its rulers, and brethren, should give law to all the churches of the universe.

6. By what authority is the meeting at Jerusalem

called a synod? Who were the members that composed it? Were they not the apostles, the elders, and brethren of the Church of Jerusalem *only?* Was there a single representative, either minister or lay elder, from any other church upon earth? Those who accompanied Paul and Barnabas from Antioch, were not representatives, but messengers of that church, to report the matter of fact, and receive the decision. Accordingly, the letters are in the name, not of a representative council, but of the apostles, the elders, and brethren at Jerusalem, from whom the troublesome teachers went out. How absurd would be their language, upon the supposition that there were representatives in it, from the Church of Antioch, and others. "For as much as we have heard, that certain which went out *from us.*" Could the Antioch, and other representatives, put their signatures to this letter? Could they say that they went out *from them?* They went out from the church at Jerusalem, and no one could say, "they went out *from us,*" but the church at Jerusalem. The language "went out *from us,*" plainly excludes from that assembly, all members from foreign churches.

7. As there were no representatives in this meeting, from any other church, so *all the members or brethren* of the church at Jerusalem, were admitted. What is there similar to this in Presbytery. So far from being admitted into general meetings, they have no share in the administration of the affairs of a single congregation. The minister and elders, are the sole judges, in all disputes. The people must make their mind known, by petition to church courts. Upon the supposition, that this was a representative assembly, consisting of members from the different churches of Judea, Samaria, Antioch, &c., by what authority did *the brethren* of the church at Jerusalem, take a share in the deliberations? What peculiar right had they over the brethren of all other churches, to a place in this assembly? Why did not the church at Jerusalem choose representatives, as well as the other churches? Or, if the Jerusalem brethren were to be admitted, why not all the members of all the churches, or at least, as many of them as might choose to attend?

What Presbyterian assembly is so constituted? This would destroy the balance of power. The admission of the brethren of the church at Jerusalem, plainly shows that it was not a representative assembly.

8. This was an appeal to inspired authority, which, in after ages, could be imitated only by appealing to the apostolical writings. The message was to the apostles, and to the elders, who were men endowed with the gifts of the Spirit. This was nothing else than our appeal to the Scriptures. The apostolical writings were not then in existence; the apostles themselves were in the room of the New Testament. There was no other possible way of deciding the dispute. The Scriptures that were then in being had nothing *express* upon the subject. But what question can now arise in any church, which the Scripture cannot determine. They contain a full and perfect rule of faith and practice. This question is settled for ever, and the decision is a part of Scripture. Never can the same, or a similar, again occur. Paul and Barnabas, it is true, were at Antioch; but they, in some sort, were esteemed a party, by the judaizing teachers. Besides this important question, the condition upon which the Gentiles were to be received into the church, behoved to be discussed and settled in the most public manner, that the Jews in every part of the world, might the more readily unite with them. Accordingly, it seems probable that this was the time, and this the occasion, that Paul went up to Jerusalem, by revelation—Gal. ii. 2.* The apostles might have decided the question themselves, but it behoved to be done in this manner, because it was a matter in which the Church of Jerusalem was concerned, as the false teachers had gone out from them, and because they wished, in this first church, to give a public specimen of transacting church business. This shows us, that matters of public concernment to a church, are not to be smuggled through a session, but conducted in the presence, and by the consent, of the whole brethren. Though, then, it affords not a precedent for one church to appeal to

---

* See Innes's Reasons, page 39.

another, yet this portion of Scripture will, to the end of the world, be useful to direct us in transacting church business.

9. The decision of the church at Jerusalem was the issue of the infallible interpretation of Scripture, and the voice of God in the previous conversion of the Gentiles. Peter argues, that if God had already given them conversion without circumcision, the matter must be already determined, as they were really already saved, when they were converted. If, then, circumcision, or the Mosaic law, had been necessary, they must have received it before conversion. He argues from their belief, that the Gentiles and themselves should be saved in the same manner, that is, wholly through the Lord Jesus Christ, which could not be the case, if they must be circumcised. James proves the same, by an inference from a passage of one of the prophets. Now, none can plead this as a precedent for any body of men to settle controverted matters for others, who cannot plead the gift of infallible interpretation of Scripture.

10. If the apostles presumed not to give their decision, without giving such reasons, upon which it was founded, how arrogant are those assemblies, who make their own opinion of expediency the law of every individual! Were such assemblies of God's own appointing, yet, if their proceedings are not directed by the Scriptures; if they cannot plead the sanction of the Scriptures for every decision, their acts would be invalid. Let synods apply this criterion to their decrees, and it will at once sweep away all their *prudential regulations, and human expedients*, and every act that cannot plead express Scripture. It will not be enough, that such a thing is the "*mind of this synod*," but that such a thing is the mind of Scripture, the voice of God.

11. No body of men can plead this as a precedent to determine in matters of religion for others, who cannot preface their decree with: "It seemed good unto us, and *to the Holy Ghost*." Without this, their decision is as invalid as an act of parliament without the sanction of the king.

12. Whatever be the divine model of church government, it is in no measure invested with a power of legislation. The question of a right to make laws according to circumstances, for the government of Christ's church, and the inquiry into the divine form of its government, are entirely distinct. Whether Episcopacy, Presbytery, or Independency be of God, to none of them can belong a right to enact new laws, any more than to promulgate new doctrines. The business of church rulers is not to make laws, but to execute the laws which they find enacted by Christ, in the New Testament. If an individual Independent church, were to take upon itself to enact laws, draw up a plan of rules and regulations for their government, and worship, I would have the same objections to it, that I have to Presbytery. To suppose a liberty to enact laws or regulations, according to the exigence of circumstances, is to arraign the competency of Christ, as the King of the church, and a declaration that he hath left the code of laws imperfect. Executive and legislative authority, even in civil affairs, are entirely distinct, and in the best governments, are lodged in different hands. The Parliament enacts laws, and the civil magistracy executes them. As well might the civil magistrates of a county meet to frame laws, in imitation of the Parliament, as church rulers plead the right of making laws, because the inspired apostles of God did so. Church rulers are to execute the laws which the apostles enacted. Every new law is an act of treason against Christ, and an attempt to rob him of the most valuable prerogative of his crown. How astonishing is it to hear men arguing so warmly, that Christ would not leave his church without a form of government, who suppose that he has left it without a sufficient code of laws! Surely it is as necessary to have divine laws for the government of Christ's church, as a divine plan of executing those laws. If the laws are human, what avails it that the plan of government be agreeable to the Scripture model? Were we then to allow that the plan of church government, by synods, &c., &c., was the true one, still their business would be very different from what it is. They would not

meet as legislators, but as jurors, to judge of the *application* of Christ's laws. Suppose, for instance, that a member of their communion was charged with being an extortioner, a reviler, a drunkard, &c., there is an express law of Christ, that he should become a subject of discipline. Now, their business would be, to judge the offender by the law of Christ, examine proofs, and determine whether or not the charge was fairly applicable. But it happens, that this rule is given to the brethren of an individual church, and not to a synod or Presbytery.

But the very idea of a right of legislation in the Church of Christ, supposes infallibility in the legislators. To suppose that Christ would give a commission to men, to make laws, and a command to his people to obey them, while at the same time, he would leave such men without infallible direction, is monstrously absurd. If synods are fallible, they may enact sinful laws, and enforce them in the awful name, and by the authority of the Lord Jesus Christ. If they are not infallible, why do they enforce their laws, as if they were infallible? Do they not enforce the smallest law they enact, with the same rigour they could do a law of God? Nay, it is very possible to break many of the laws of God with impunity, while a law of synod or Presbytery must be inviolable. If an individual approve not of any law, the only redress he has, is to separate. He has no liberty to act upon his own convictions. Their opinion of expediency must be his guide. Now, if they are not infallibly right, why do they not leave individuals to act according to their own convictions? Is not this, to " teach for doctrines the commandments of men?"

Upon the whole, in the 15th chap. of Acts, we have no precedent for any foreign interference among the churches of Christ. The distinguishing features in this assembly, are not to be found, nor ever can be found, in any assembly on earth. If it be asked, of what use is this relation to us, if it does not warrant us to decide differences in a similar way, I would answer, that whenever a text of Scripture is so explained, as to be rendered useless to after ages, I readily grant, that it certainly must be a forced explanation. But have we not here a precedent for appealing to the apostles, in all our controversies, as the Church of Antioch did? Have we not here a precedent of applying every doctrine, and *observance*, and *rite*, and *regulation* of churches to the Word of God? If the apostles drew their conclusions from this source, shall *human prudence*, and *expedience* direct church rulers? Every tittle must be brought "to the law and to the testimony, whoever speaks not agreeable to this, it is because there is no light in them." Have we not here, an admirable model for the transaction of all church business. The question could, indeed, only be determined by apostles; but as it was an affair in which the church at Jerusalem was concerned, and to give us a living model for transacting church business, the apostles consider the matter in conjunction with the whole church. What a beautiful picture does it give us of a church meeting! It is not a minister and session, nor the ministers and lay-elders of a district, but the apostles, elders, or pastors, and brethren. Whenever the pastors and brethren of a particular church come together now, they must have the apostles in their hands, by whose writings they are to conduct all their affairs.

CHAPTER V.

OF THE OFFICE OF LAY ELDERS.

HAVING, in the last chapter, examined the pretensions of Presbyterians, as founded on the relation contained in the 15th chap. of the Acts of the Apostles, I intend, in this, to inquire into the validity of the office of lay-elders. Presbyterians themselves are not agreed, either as to the foundation, extent, or prerogatives of this office; a circumstance that will go far, in the judgment of every unprejudiced inquirer, to prove that the office is not scriptural. As to the Scripture authority of lay-elders, some refer us to the office of deacon. "Though the name is not scriptural (say they), yet the office is." But here I would remark, that the names are not more different than the offices. A Scripture deacon is an officer in the Church of Christ, for managing its temporal concerns, and attending to the wants of the poor brethren. He has no concern in the ruling of the church, more than the rest of the brethren. A lay-elder is compounded of a New Testament deacon, the half of a New Testament elder or pastor, as he is a church ruler, and a part of the office of an apostle, as a legislator, to make laws for the church. In the superior courts, he is looked upon by some as a representative of the people; by others as the representative of his own order. In either view, his office is derived from our ideas of civil policy; for there is not the shadow of any such representation in the Word of God. It is absurd in the extreme, to found his office on that of the Scripture deacon, seeing it extends so much further. If he is the same as the deacon, let him do the deacon's office only. Besides, if he be the deacon, why has he been called elder? Has not the father the best right to give the name to the child? Is not the Spirit of him who instituted the office, the best judge of the most fitting name? Especially as the name was appropriated to another order in the church, why was *it* chosen? If men thought that they could give a more proper and decent name to this office, than the Spirit of God had done, which is not a very modest supposition, why did they take that which he had assigned to pastors? Has not the tendency of this been to mislead the English reader, and make him believe, that where he meets the word elder, in the New Testament, the Presbyterian elder was intended, and not the pastor. This has been one of the most successful artifices of priestcraft in all ages. But there are others who pretend to find both name and office in the New Testament, and produce as their authority, 1 Tim. v. 17—" Let the elders that rule well, be counted worthy of double honour, especially they who labour in word and doctrine." " Here (say they) is an evident distinction between ruling and teaching elders. There must be some elders to rule, and others to teach." To this I answer—

1. Allowing the Presbyterian explanation of this text, in its utmost latitude, what does it make? Granting that there should be a body of lay-elders to join with the preaching elders, in ruling a church, does this give any countenance to a church session as a body of legislators, to make laws, rules, and regulations for the congregation? Their being church rulers, does not constitute them church legislators. Upon this supposition, their business would be to carry the laws of Christ into effect, not to make laws. Neither would this give any countenance to a minister and session, exclusively judging of the application of discipline, and engrossing the whole power of the church into their own hands. Whether the elders of a particular church be all pastors, or some ruling, and others teaching elders, to neither would belong the sole right of judging when the laws of Christ were to be applied. If a brother was accused, the whole church would judge him according to the law of Christ; and if he is found guilty, the business of church rulers is to execute the law of Christ, which the church has judged

applicable; just as a judge pronounces the verdict found by the jury. But a church session is not only a parliament to make laws, but a jury to judge of the application of both their own and Christ's laws. The brethren are entirely excluded. They may lodge a complaint, or appear as a witness, but in judging of the guilt or innocence of the accused, they have no share. I do not stay here to show that this is contrary to the apostolical commands, in which the whole church is intrusted and charged with judging of the application of discipline. This I intend to show in another place. What I would observe here, is, that according to their own interpretation of this text, there is no foundation for the legislative or exclusive judicial authority of church sessions.

2. Allowing, from this text, an order of ruling elders, distinct from teaching elders, this gives no countenance to a body of what are called lay-elders; that is, men not invested with the pastoral office. Such ruling elders would be as really pastors, bishops, ministers, &c., as the preaching elders. The office of a preaching elder would not be superior to that of the ruling elder. The ruling elder would be a pastor of the church, invested with the pastoral character, in as full a manner as the preaching elder. The only legitimate conclusion that could be drawn from this interpretation, would be, that in every church there should be two orders of ministers, the one for ruling, and the other for preaching; and that neither of these had a right to interfere in the department of the other. The preaching elder was not to rule, any more than the ruling elder was to preach. The preaching elder, then, should not preside in the session, nay, he should have no seat in it, any more than the ruling elder should have in the pulpit. If the one is only to rule, the other is only to preach. If the one must not mount the pulpit, neither must the other sit in church-court. All then that can be fairly inferred from this interpretation, is, that in the pastoral office, there are two distinct departments, which should not interfere with each other; that those appointed to rule, should rule; and those appointed to preach, should preach; which, instead of

serving, would overthrow, from the foundation, the whole Presbyterian system. If, then, we should allow that there is in this text, an order of ruling elders, distinct from another order of preaching elders, still such ruling elders would be pastors or bishops, and nothing a-kin to Presbyterian elders. Nay, the ruling elders would be more eminently, if not exclusively, the bishops or overseers. Oversight surely belongs rather to the ruler, than the preacher.

3. Is it possible that two orders so different as that of ministers and lay-elders, should be called invariably in Scripture, by the same name? Is this like the perspicuity of the Bible? Is it probable, that when the New Testament writers employ so many words to denote the same office, as bishop, presbyter, shepherd, &c., they could not afford a distinct name for the office of lay-elder, if it was apostolical? Is this agreeable to the use of any language, upon any subject? Especially, is it agreeable to the genius of the philosophic language of Greece, where every shade of difference in idea, is marked by a different word, expressive of it? But the English reader of the most common understanding, must be convinced that it is impossible for the Greek word πρεσβυτερος, to denote two so widely different officers from the use of our own word elder. Though this is the exact translation of the Greek word, and in the estimation of Presbyterians, must include both minister and lay-elder, yet to avoid confusion, it has been appropriated by them to denote the latter only. What Presbyterian speaks promiscuously of ministers and lay-elders by the common name elders? Or who would understand him if he did? Yet such undefined, indeterminate language, they scruple not to put into the mouth of the Holy Ghost. If ever they use the word elder to denote the minister, they are obliged to prefix the word *lay* to it, when attributed to the Presbyterian elder, to prevent obscurity. Now, if we cannot talk in English of ministers and Presbyterian elders by the same name, is it possible that the Scriptures should be guilty of this obscurity?

4. Granting that this text does constitute two orders of elders, then there will be three orders of officers in

every church, and the Presbyterians want the third. They have not the deacon. "Yes (say they), our elder is the deacon." But upon what authority do they combine offices, which the apostles kept distinct. There is incontestibly an order of deacons; if there be two orders of elders, there should be three distinct orders in every church. No man hath authority to combine any two of them into one, any more than to make a new order over the rest. If it be said, that the office of the lay-elder and that of the deacon are the same, I have already shown that they are widely different. The office of a deacon is to take care of the poor; whereas, if there be a distinct order of ruling elders, their office must be to rule the church. Is there any evidence in Scripture, that these two offices were combined into one? The office of the deacon is in itself no more connected with ruling, than with preaching. To rule in the church, and to take charge of the poor, are offices distinct in themselves, and separated in the New Testament.

5. If there had been two orders of elders, so distinct as that of lay and preaching elders, is it possible that their offices and qualifications should be included in the same description? In describing the office of the elder, and his qualifications, no notice is taken of two orders, one as requiring a different kind of qualifications from the other. They are called upon, without exception, to feed the flock, take the oversight of it, &c.; and are all required to be διδακτικός, "fit to teach," which, as Dr. Campbell has observed, could hardly be the case, if some of them were to have no concern in teaching. This candid inquirer has given up this text, and thinks it is too trivial a circumstance, upon which to found so material a distinction. It is not said, that a preaching elder must have such and such qualifications, and do so and so, but *the elder*, which must include every distinction of elders. Besides, the words elder and bishop are perfectly interchangeable, constantly applied to the same officers, as all Presbyterians will allow. Now, if there be an order of lay-elders, there must be also an order of lay-bishops; that is, *men who have the pastoral office, yet are no pastors.*

6. Commentators seem generally agreed, and the 18th verse absolutely requires that τιμη, here translated "honour," signifies the *honourable maintenance of the ministers of the gospel*. The apostle proves that they are worthy of this τιμη, from the law of Moses, respecting the ox employed in treading out the corn, and from the words of our Lord, with respect to those engaged in preaching his Word. Now, the argument drawn from this, goes directly to show that all those elders, spoken of in the 17th verse, are worthy of honourable support. It does not indeed require that a church is, in every situation, to support all its labourers. Some may not need it; the church may be so poor that it cannot support more than one pastor. There is nothing to prevent it from using the labours of some who support themselves by lawful industry. But the text undoubtedly implies, that all elders are *worthy* of support, and if they need, and the church can give it, it is their right. Do Presbyterians think it their duty to support their elders, or will any one say, that they are worthy of it? If not, they cannot be the elders of which the apostle speaks. Besides, the 18th verse proves incontestibly, that all the elders spoken of in the 17th verse, have the same pastoral character, and are employed in the same work. They are all "treaders out of the corn," all "labourers worthy of reward." How do Presbyterian elders "tread out the corn?" In what manner do the most conscientious of them "labour so as to be worthy of reward?" These figures represent the elders as labouring constantly in the work of the Gospel, and having that for their employment, as the ox was daily employed in early days, and till the present time, in some countries, in "treading out the corn," and as a labourer is employed, not occasionally, but constantly in his labour. Should it be said, that the illustration in the 18th verse, is applicable only to the latter part of the 17th verse, I answer, that beside the necessity of referring it to the whole verse, the texts quoted by the apostle, would not be relevant in that view. They go to prove the propriety of support in general, and not a superiority of support.

7. Hitherto I have granted, that this text does create

two orders of elders; and even on that supposition, have shown that this constitutes two different orders of pastors in every church, not a separate order of what are called lay-elders. I will now endeavour to show, that the text neither proves nor admits a distinction of order among the elders spoken of. The opposition is not between ruling elders and preaching elders, but in the first part of the verse, between those who discharge the office well *in general*, and those who are particularly employed and distinguished for talents and labour in that difficult, important, and laborious branch of the office, the preaching continually to large public assemblies. In every apostolical church, that was perfectly organised, there was a plurality of elders or pastors, of different gifts. Some were distinguished as public speakers, others as church rulers, others for a talent of private exhortation, peculiarly fitted to converse with the saints, on the state of their souls, and to pour the balm of consolation into the wounded spirit. Now, each of these sustained the whole of the pastoral office or character, and might occasionally be employed in any part of it, while each was usually employed in that department of his office, for which his talents, and his temper, fitted him. The advantages which would thus accrue to the church, are obvious and admirable. It enjoyed this diversity of gifts, while at the same time, if any of the elders were absent, or should die, or that it could not procure, or support for some time, as many elders or pastors as were necessary, any one of them could officiate in the peculiar department of any other. Churches which have not this plurality of pastors, and diversity of gifts, are not aware of the disadvantage under which they labour. At the same time, some congregations which have a plurality of pastors, do not seem to know how to use them. They do not assign their pastors, each the peculiar province for which he is best qualified, but each statedly labours in every part of the office, alternately. This plurality of elders, is rather suited to the indolence of the labourer, than the edification of the church. This being the case, the reason of the injunction of the text is obvious and important. All such elders are worthy of "honourable maintenance;" those who are distinguished in their office, have a right to a double portion; especially those who are peculiarly and usually employed in preaching. This requires peculiar, and perhaps rarer talents; much more time, study, and expense to qualify them for the office; has much greater labour and fatigue; incurs more expense, by frequent excursions; exposes much more to public censure and odium; and requires much more intense application to furnish the mind, so as to be a workman that needeth not to be ashamed, rightly dividing the word of truth. To discharge this part of the office in a proper manner, requires a life solely devoted to it. Such is my view of this text; now to confirm it.

The word translated "rule," is by no means exclusively applicable to that department of the pastoral office called ruling. Προεστῶς is rather a military than a civil officer: rather a commander in the field than a president in an assembly. Προεδρος would be the most proper word for the latter. Accordingly, in the Athenian council of 500, the seven of the Prytanes chosen by lot to preside every week, were called προεδροι; and the president of the day was called επιστατης. This is a too peaceful and inactive office to give a name to Christ's officers. I know not that they are ever so called in the New Testament, though they early assumed this title. But προεστῶς is a word which fully expresses their arduous, dangerous, and honourable office. It signifies an officer who goes before his men, and stands in the front of the battle. He encourages them by his example and exhortations, and leads them into action. Officers have the command and the care of the army; train and discipline the soldiers; and keep them to their duty. They take care to supply them with provisions, and prepare them for battle, by military speeches. Such an officer is the elder in the Church of Christ. Like a military officer, he trains and disciplines his troops; supplies them with wholesome provisions; rules them by the laws of Christ; instructs them in the will of their king; and prepares them for battle, by his public preaching. I apprehend, then, that the word προεστωτες here, is not to be referred exclusively, to any one part of the pastoral office, but to the office in general. It means, the elders who discharge, in an eminent manner, the duty of an officer in the army of Christ, and preaching is as essential a part of this, as ruling. That προεστώς refers to the office in general, is farther evident, from 1 Thess. v. 12.—where the same persons who are said to labour among them, and to admonish them, are called also προϊσταμενους. Indeed, I am astonished that any person who has ever looked into the Greek Testament, should think that the προεστώτες were an order inferior to preachers. There is not a higher word to denote pastor, in all the Word of God. They are Christ's military officers. Accordingly, they are called also, Heb. xiii. 17.—ἡγουμενοι, or military leaders. Agreeably to this, we find, that when one of the elders began to be distinguished above his colleagues, he assumed these very appellations as the most honourable. He exclusively appropriated to himself, προεστώς, and ηγουμενος, as well as επισκωπος, or bishop. But especially, can there be any thing more unfit to the character of military officers, than an order of lay-elders?

My sense of the passage, may be illustrated by a simile. "Let the kings who rule well, be accounted worthy of double honour, especially those who distinguish themselves as the protectors of religious liberty." Here ruling well, refers to the whole kingly office, and the word "especially" distinguishes a particular department of the duty of a king. "Let virtuous and distinguished legislators, be esteemed worthy of double honour, especially those who labour for the abolition of the slave trade." Who would infer from this, that members of Parliament were each confined to a particular department. Each member has a right to speak and vote upon every subject, though his time and talents may be chiefly employed on his favourite object.

Besides, if I am not greatly mistaken, grammar requires that οι κοπιῶντες have προεστῶτες πρεςβύτεροι, and not merely πρεσβύτεροι, for its antecedent. The phraseology is οἱ καλῶς προεστῶτες πρεσβύτεροι, and not οἱ πρεσβύτεροι οἱ καλῶς προεστωτες. But common sense requires that the προεστῶτες πρεσβύτεροι, include the κοπιωντες εν λογω και διδασκαλια. If a general, after a victory, would write thus to the secretary at war, " the officers merit the highest praise, especially the general officers," he would write sense. But how ridiculous would it be to say, " the subaltern officers merit the highest praise, especially the general officers." In the first instance, the word "officers" includes the general officers; but in the second, the general officers are not included among the subaltern officers. Now, this is exactly what the Presbyterian interpretation of this text makes the apostles say, " Let ruling elders be counted worthy of honour, especially the preaching elders." Μαλιστα is properly used, when a part is distinguished out of the whole; or one out of a number. Compare this passage, with 2 Tim. iv. 13.—" Bring with you the cloak, and the books, especially the parchments." Here, the generic word books includes the parchments, as a particular sort of the books which he had desired him to bring. But how ridiculous would it have been to have said, " Bring the cloak, especially the parchments."

Thus have I examined the meaning of this much disputed portion of Scripture. I have first endeavoured to show, that granting Presbyterians their own interpretation of this text, and that it fully establishes an order of lay-elders, or an order of rulers in the church, who are not pastors, that even this did not give a church session any authority to judge in all matters for the church or congregation. Even in this case, the whole church should judge, and those officers carry the result into execution. Again, that granting the exclusive management of church affairs to the session, gave it no authority to legislate, as the whole church, or the united voice of all the churches upon earth, have no right to make the slightest alteration, amendment, or addition with respect to the laws of Christ's Church. Further, that granting a distinction of order in elders to be established from this verse, it would make two orders of pastors, and not a distinct order of lay-elders. And, lastly, that a distinction of order of any kind, is neither necessary, probable, nor possible, from this verse. It constitutes, indeed, a plurality of pastors, in every perfectly organised church, who, being of different gifts, should be usually employed in the department best suited to each; that there should be a gradation of support according to talents, zeal, and diligence; and that the highest is due to those who are distinguished *for labouring in word and doctrine*. This plurality of elders or pastors in a church, is called (1 Tim. iv. 14), the Presbytery or Eldership. The modern signification of the word Presbytery, as consisting of the ministers and representative lay-elders of the congregations of a whole district, is not known in Scripture, nor in all the first ages of Christianity.*

* Chrysostom supposed the Presbytery spoken of (1 Tim. iv. 14), to have been a synod of bishops. To what extravagance will men run, who give themselves up to a party, and take their opinions from their sect, and not from the Bible!

CHAPTER VI.

OF INDEPENDENCY.

I HAVE an objection against imposing names of *human invention* upon *the things of the Spirit*. When I use the words Independency and Independents, for that form of church government, instituted by the apostles, and those who now embrace it, I would be understood to do it, not of choice, but of necessity. The disciples of Christ are properly called *Christians, saints*, or *brethren*, and an assembly of these, for the purpose of enjoying the ordinances of Christ, according to his appointment, is called a *church*. Now, these are the words I would always wish to use to denote the same objects; but it has happened that some of them have been so abused and prostituted to other significations, that it is impossible to use these plain Scripture words without obscurity. There is now the Church of Rome, the Church of England, the Church of Scotland, the Church of Secession, &c., &c., &c. In speaking therefore of a church formed on the model of the apostolical churches, we are obliged to call it an *Independent* Church, to distinguish it from the others, which have usurped the name. Still, however, we use this, not as the name of Christ's Church, but of the particular mode of the government of an apostolical church, to mark its distinctive feature. The apostles had no occasion to use this, or any other word of the same nature, for the same purpose, because no different form of government had been erected. It is obvious, then, that this use of the word *Independency*, is very different from sacrament, eucharist, altar, clergy, and a multitude of other such names, which the wisdom of men has imposed upon the ordinances of God.

That the government of Christ's appointment, is what is called Independent, is obvious from the rule which he gave for the settling of private offences among his disciples. Matt. xviii. 15–18.—"Moreover, if thy brother shall trespass against thee, go and tell him his fault, between thee and him alone: if he shall hear thee, thou hast gained thy brother. But if he will not hear *thee, then* take with thee one or two more, that in the mouth of one or two witnesses, every word may be established. And if he shall neglect to hear them, tell *it* unto the church: but if he neglect to hear the church, let him be unto thee as an heathen man, and a publican." Here the last appeal is to the church. He does not say, if he does not hear the church, take him to the Presbytery, and if he does not hear the Presbytery, take him to the Synod, &c., but if he hear not the church, "let him be unto thee as an heathen man, and a publican." I know, indeed, that various subterfuges have been invented to evade the force of this plain Scripture. Every sect has attempted to find its own discipline in this passage, whilst individuals, to apologise for what they cannot justify, have attempted to darken its meaning so as to make it of no practical use. The multiplicity of interpretations, in the opinion of Dr. Stillingfleet, is an argument to prove that it is totally inexplicable; in my opinion it proves only what is proved by the variety of sentiments on every other point in Scripture, the perversity, the selfishness, or the prejudice of professing Christians. What! has the Lord Jesus given a precept, in a case of such importance, and of such frequent occurrence, which cannot be understood? Did he wish to be, or could he not avoid being unintelligible? Must the Holy One of Israel speak with the darkness and evasion of an heathen oracle? If he did not mean to be understood, why did he speak? If he meant to be understood, why did he not speak in intelligible language? If we cannot find out who are the divinely appointed arbitrators of our differences, he might as well have said nothing on the subject. What an insult upon the Holy Ghost to represent his language to be so vague and indeterminate, that it cannot be understood? Christ has said "tell it to the church;" is there no way of coming at his meaning? Has the word *church* no determinate meaning in the New Testament? But Dr. Stillingfleet is of opinion, that if the discipline Christ has appointed, be executed, it is not material by whom. Is it then the same thing, whether a law be enacted by the lawfully appointed legislators, or by any other body of self-constituted men? or that a criminal be tried by a lawful judge and jury, or by men who assume the right of judgment, without the countenance of lawful authority? If Christ has appointed any particular referees, it is as really a breach of his injunction to appoint any other, as it would be totally to neglect that instance of discipline. But is there any native necessary obscurity in the precept, arising from the promiscuous use of the word *church*, in the New Testament? If it is now in any measure obscure, it has been rendered so, not from the ambiguity of the Scripture use of the word, but from its prostituted application in modern acceptation, and the sophistry, and subtleties of interested, prejudiced, or bigoted men; we find no difficulty in the passage until we hear the forced explanations of it given by controvertists, and our mind begins to be distracted, and the subject obscured by the smoke of their unhallowed fires.

I lay it down, then, as an axiom, that Christ meant some *determinate thing* by the word *church*, and that there must be sufficient evidence in the New Testament to lead the humble, teachable inquirer into that meaning. Christ must have spoken intelligible language. Now, to investigate the Scripture-use of the word *church*.

In every language there are two different processes recognised, which affect the signification of words, appropriation and extension. The one confines them to a part of their original territories, the other extends them a little beyond their natural limits. This is not peculiar to the language of Scripture, but is practised in treating of all the arts and sciences, and the whole business of life. Thus the word angel literally signifies a messenger, and is not naturally confined to any description of messengers. But the Bible hath in a manner appropriated that word to denote an order of beings, whose employment is that of messengers of the Most

High, sent forth to minister to the heirs of salvation. And though it may occasionally, even in Scripture, claim its natural rights, being sometimes used for other messengers, yet it is the *appropriated name* of that order of beings called angels. The same may be said of the words *apostle, elder, bishop,* &c. Sometimes they are appropriated upon particular subjects or departments, while they enjoy the full extent of their signification upon others; and sometimes the same word is differently appropriated upon different subjects. Thus, while the words angel, apostle, &c., are usually confined to a particular province in Scripture, they have unbounded license in profane authors, of the same date; and thus when men use the word minister, conversing upon political subjects, it is immediately understood that they mean the first minister of state. But if they are conversing on religion, it is as readily understood to be *the minister of the congregation.* On the other hand, sometimes a word will come through time to exceed its natural boundaries, and be extended to include ideas not necessarily, nor naturally inherent in it. Thus χειροτονεω, literally signifies to vote by holding up the hand, and was used in the popular assemblies of Athens in contradistinction to the vote by scrutiny, which was denoted by ψηφιζω, from ψηφος, the pebble used by the voters. But in an advanced period of the history of this word, we find that it sometimes dropped the principal idea altogether, and was extended to denote election in any manner, and even the conferring of an office, not by election but individual nomination. Our language has recognised the same abusive principle, in the words man-midwife, head-pleurisy, &c. Now, to apply this reasoning to the point in dispute. We are to enquire what εκκλησια literally signifies; what it was originally applied to; what it came to be applied to in the process of its history; what is its use in other instances in Scripture; how it is used in profane authors of the same date; whether in the New Testament, it hath been appropriated, or extended; and if appropriated, to what? Proceeding thus, we shall find, that in the New Testament it is invariably used, either for an individual congregation, or the whole community of Christians.

Εκκλησια literally signifies an assembly *called out* from others, and is used among the Greeks, particularly the Athenians, for their popular assemblies summoned by their chief magistrate, and in which none but *citizens* had a right to sit. By inherent power it may be applied to any body of men *called out*, and *assembled in one place*. If ever it loses the ideas of *calling out*, and *assembling*, it loses its principal features, and its primitive use. I will not say, that by the operation of the abusive principle I have described, it might not have come to lose even both, after a length of time from its first introduction; but this I say, that I no where find it in profane writers, nor in the Scriptures speaking of civil affairs, to have lost either, but especially the latter. Nor will I be driven from my position by the use of this word in the 19th chap. of Acts. That assembly, however tumultuous, irregular, and unlawful it may have been, was a *meeting of the citizens called together* by the silversmiths. The craftsmen were *called together* (verse 25), by Demetrius, who, inflamed by his speech, burst out into intemperate acclamations to their goddess Diana. The rest of the citizens were roused and assembled by their noise, and adopting their zeal, though many of them knew not the cause, they rushed into the theatre—the very place of public deliberation. Though, then, it was an irregular, lawless assembly, it was nothing a-kin to an English mob, but rather like a parliament assembling, being summoned, not by the king, but by some incendiary among themselves. Still more strongly may it be affirmed, that it is no where used by profane writers to denote any body of men, but in their *assembled* capacity; they are called εκκλησια only as *assembled*.

Such being the origin and use of this word among the Greeks, to what may it be legitimately applied when used in sacred things? It may signify any *assembly called out* from the world, and *united in Christ*. Agreeably to this, whenever it is used in Scripture in a sacred sense, that is, as applicable to believers, we find that it is invariably appropriated to an individual assembly of Christians, meeting to enjoy the ordinances of Christ,* or the Christian community in general. Whenever the apostles made a number of converts in any place, they separated them from the congregation, by forming them into an εκκλησια, or church. And just as in the Athenian assemblies none but citizens could sit or vote, so none but the citizens of the new Jerusalem were allowed to join themselves to this company. As in the Parliament many may be present to hear, though none but senators speak or vote; so in a church of Christ, many are present to hear the Gospel of salvation, but none are admitted as members of the εκκλησια, but those who are first by that Gospel made citizens of heaven. But with equal propriety may this word be applied to all the Christians in heaven and earth, as assembled in Jesus. Nor does this application stretch it a whit beyond its natural and intrinsic meaning. It is as literally and as truly applied to the one as to the other. All the saints on earth, and all the saints in heaven, are assembled in him, as really as the branches of a vine are united in the trunk, the stones of a building upon the foundation, or the members of the body with the head. With the strictest truth all Christians may be said to be already "in heavenly places in Christ." This double application of the word is neither foreign nor forced, incorrect nor indistinct. When it is used indefinitely, it applies to the community of believers assembled in Christ; when it is used with respect to an individual church, which is its most general application, the context, or the nature of the circumstances, gives sufficient intimation. Let any one take the trouble to run over all the places where it is found in the New Testament, and I will be bold to say, he will not find a single text, which will not fairly explain on this hypothesis. The cases where it may occur in the civil or unappropriated sense, are not accompanied with the smallest difficulty, the context, or a note of appropriation as "Church of Christ,"

---

* Where this word is used, for the Christians of a family, it is rather a confirmation of this than an exception. Every Christian family, meeting morning and evening for worship, may be properly considered a little church.

&c., sufficiently marking the difference. Those who, from this circumstance, would argue the impossibility of ascertaining the meaning of the word church in Matt. xviii. 17., and elsewhere, will find the same difficulty in the words apostle, angel, and innumerable others. Indeed the admission of this principle, and I see it admitted, and acted upon, by some very ingenious men, would involve, in impenetrable darkness, the clearest point in theology. If it be maintained, that the meaning of a word so important, so frequently used in the epistles, could not be ascertained, why should not this be the case with others? Were such a principle established in criticism, I have no hesitation in saying, that there is not an ancient author could be understood; that there is not a passage so clear in any author, in any language, upon any subject, which could not be so perplexed by the ingenuity of a sophist, that the ablest critic could not unravel it. Critics would be ashamed to reason thus on a passage in Homer or Sophocles. Grant only to the inspired writers, what will be granted to all—that they had a meaning in their words, and wrote to be understood, and it will be our fault if we cannot understand them.

Having stated the literal meaning, the profane and sacred application of the word εκκλησια, let us next examine the claims of its modern* acceptations. It is quite a cameleon. It is as various in its meaning, as the necessities of each party require. Sometimes it is a church session; sometimes an individual church; sometimes a classical Presbytery; sometimes a synod; sometimes a general assembly; sometimes church rulers; sometimes all the churches of a province or kingdom. Truly, if the Scripture gives ground for all these, it is more dark and perplexing than was ever an answer of the Sybil. Is not the bare statement a refutation of the fact? and the supposition a calumny on the oracles of God? But the practice of Presbyterians themselves, is a complete refutation of this hypothesis. They do not speak promiscuously of all their assemblies

---

* I call them modern, because they are later than the New Testament.

by the name church, but have a distinct name for each, as the congregation, the session, the Presbytery, the Synod, &c. Now, if each order of these courts be a church, as well as each congregation, and the collective congregations, why do they not speak of them by the Scripture name? Why have they imposed upon them names of their own invention? Evidently because they would otherwise be unintelligible. If one of their writers on church discipline was to speak of all their assemblies by the name church, without additional marks of distinction, his readers would not understand him; yet this is the very inaccuracy they charge upon the writers of the New Testament. They suppose them to speak promiscuously of the greatest variety of subordinate courts, as well as assemblies of a different nature, by the same name, without any mark of distinction to guide the reader. Now, I think this is a very fair criterion; Scripture ordinances should be sufficiently intelligible by Scripture names, without the use of any other. I believe it will be found a very just conclusion, *that the institutions which have not a name in Scripture, have not an existence in Scripture.* Let Presbyterians, then, use nothing but the Scripture names, and their doctrine of subordinate courts will be jargon. By their unnatural extension of this word, they have taken it in modern use from that which alone deserves it—the individual assemblies of the saints. Let us suppose, then, that εκκλησια might have been legitimately appropriated to denote any one of these assemblies, this appropriation will take it from all the rest. If a session is a church, then a congregation cannot be a church; if either of these be a church, then a Presbytery cannot, without confusion, be usually so denominated; and if a Presbytery is a church, then it will take that name from all inferior and superior courts. Now, if these courts be Scriptural, let their advocates produce their distinct Scriptural names. No word can have two appropriate meanings upon the same subject; εκκλησια may be a civil assembly and appropriated also to a religious assembly; but in neither civil nor religious matters can it be appropriated as the distinctive name of two different assemblies, the one subordinate to the other. It may denote a particular assembly of saints, and the community of Christians assembled in Jesus; but without confusion, it cannot be used as the appropriated name of a particular and general assembly of the same sort. This is clear from the names of civil courts. Though some of these be such as to be literally applicable to all, yet they are not so appropriated. Thus sessions, assizes, &c. Thus also in the Church of England, though each of the orders are called clergymen, yet for this very reason it could not be the appropriated distinctive name of any one of them. There is curate, rector, bishop, &c. For the same reason, though *bishop* was the common name of all Presbyters originally, yet when it was appropriated to one of the number, it was taken from all the rest. If, then, the word church be generally applicable to such a variety of assemblies, each assembly must have a distinctive name besides; to produce which out of Scripture will be rather an arduous task. Besides, in speaking particularly of each of these assemblies, the common name could not be used, any more than the name clergyman would distinguish a bishop from a Presbyter. When our Lord says, then "tell it to the church;" if he intends Presbyterian ecclesiastical courts, to which does he refer? If to the session, then all higher appeals are cut off; for if the offending brother will not " hear the church, let him be as an heathen man and a publican;" if it means a general synod or assembly, then all inferior courts are cut off. But if *church* be also the Scripture name of an individual assembly of saints, consisting of pastors and church members, is not the obscurity still increased? Whether must the congregation or the session be appealed to?

I have hitherto combated this multifarious application of the word, upon the supposition that it was equally proper to any one of the things signified. But I have objections against the propriety of applying it either to church rulers, or the associated churches of a province or kingdom, both from the meaning of the word and its original application, as well as its use in Scripture. According to the intrinsic ideas contained in εκκλησια, the churches of a province or kingdom could not be so called, because they are never assembled. Now this would be *an assembly, never assembled*. Should it be said that they are present in their representatives, as the nation may be said to be present in the parliament (besides that, this is too figurative for a distinctive or appropriated name), then private individuals can no more be called members of the Church of Scotland, &c., than private subjects members of parliament. None are members of an assembly, but those actually possessing a right to sit in that assembly. A national or provincial church, in this view, consists of church rulers alone, or rather a selection of church rulers. Besides, church is used in Scripture, according to its literal signification, for an assembly of saints *actually* assembled; it would not therefore be used in such a loose sense in the first stages of its history. Words may come to lose their leading idea, but it is always by the operation of time, and change of circumstances. Add to this, that the Greeks did not use it for representative assemblies; but assemblies in which all the citizens had a right to be present. None were represented, but the members who composed the assembly. Children, females, and slaves were not represented. This last objection lies equally against church rulers being at any time exclusively called *the church*. Εκκλησια was a popular assembly, distinguished from συνκλησια, an assembly of nobles or senators. It seems very clear that this latter would be the most appropriate name for a court of church rulers: I freely acknowledge, that the literal ideas contained in the word εκκλησια might be applicable to a court of church rulers, but it would be upon a principle different from its usual application among the Athenians, as well as its other acknowledged applications in Scripture. A church of Christ is so called, because it consists of members called and separated from the world by the Gospel of Christ, and united in the enjoyment of his ordinances. But if a court of church rulers were so called, it would be, not because they were called out of the world, and united in the service of Christ, but called out from their brethren to legislate for, and govern them. Now, such a use of the word would be nothing a-kin to the other. They would not be the same word, though composed of the same letters. Between the particular and general use of the word church, the leading ideas are common; both are called out of the world by the Gospel, separated from it, and assembled in Christ. But between these and the word as signifying church rulers, there is no resemblance. To appropriate a word for a double purpose upon the same subject, by a process so different, is altogether unexampled. Neither is this agreeable to the principle that generally operates in language, to extend and diversify the signification of words. They are usually correctly and unambiguously applied at first; variety of signification grows by abuse and time, as a fact related by many individuals will be known in different countries, with a loss or addition of circumstances. Add to this, that in a new science or art, when an author is obliged to borrow and appropriate a word, he doth so generally agreeably to its natural import and approved use in the language from which it is taken. If, then, our Lord had taken εκκλησια to denote an individual assembly of saints, he would have taken συνκλησια for a court of church rulers, if he had instituted such a court.

But what saith the Scripture? This must finally decide the pretensions of these different claimants. Is there a single passage in which this word must be acknowledged to have any of those significations I combat? Does it occur in any place where it plainly refers to a court of church rulers, or to a number of churches under an associated government? Are not all the passages in which it is said to be so used as undecided as the present? Upon what principle, then, of fair criticism can it be argued? If they could produce any one occurrence of it, in which it must incontestibly be so understood, there might be some colour of ground so to understand it in others, though used with less perspicuity. But without an acknowledged foundation, they never can raise a superstructure. If the word church was in any one place explained to be a representative assembly, and an association of the churches of a kingdom, they might plead such a sense here with efficacy. But if it is never so explained, never can it be so interpreted here. On the other hand we can produce texts innumerable, where it signifies an individual assembly of saints, and in which our opponents must and do acknowledge that it hath such a signification. We can produce a number of passages in which a church of Christ is explained to consist of the saints of a particular church. By what authority, then, can they refuse it to have such a signification here? There is not the least intimation in any part of the New Testament of a representavive government. Nothing is said about a number of church rulers being selected as an ecclesiastical council over a number of individual churches; nor any such use of the word church, as including a number of individual churches. When the inspired writers speak of a single assembly of saints, they invariably call it a church; when they speak of a number of churches, or the churches of a province or district, they do not call them a church, but churches. Thus when Paul writes to the Corinthians, he addresses the " *Church* of God, which is at Corinth ;" but when he writes to the Galatians, he addresses *the churches* of Galatia. Thus also when the Church of Jerusalem is spoken of, it is called *a church;* but when the aggregate of the individual churches of Judea and Samaria are spoken of, they are not called the Church of Judea, or the Church of Samaria, but the *churches* of Judea, and the *churches* of Samaria. Thus also *the Church* of Cenchrea, (Rom. xvi. 1), and the *churches* of Achaia ; the *Church* of Ephesus, the *Church* of Smyrna, &c. But when they are spoken of in the aggregate, it is the seven *churches* of Asia, not the *Church* of Asia (Rev. i. 4, and ii. 1, &c). I know indeed that with respect to Jerusalem and Corinth, it is alleged that the saints in those cities must have been too numerous to have assembled in one place. But I need not take up my time in showing how or where they might assemble, or in ascertaining their numbers. They are not more numerous than I wish them to have been; and the

Scripture itself refutes the objection in both instances—Acts ii. 44, 1. Cor. v. 4, and xi. 18. In these passages they are expressly shown to have met in the same place.

But if there were really any ambiguity in Matt. xviii. 17., can there be a better way of ascertaining truth than by referring to the use of it in the writings of the New Testament of a later date, thus comparing spiritual things with spiritual? Can there be a better commentary on the Gospels than the Epistles? If any thing is not fully explained, but hinted at, by Christ, where will we go for farther information, but to the apostles, who were to finish the revelation he had begun, and fully illustrate, what may be said to lie in embryo in his words? Can any thing then be a clearer commentary on Matt. xviii. 17, if it needed any, than 1 Cor. vi. 1—where Paul speaks of another similar case of discipline? Can it be supposed that the apostle would institute one way of terminating disputes, and his master another? The apostles makes the *saints* of *an individual church* at Corinth, the arbiters of civil disputes. Would he have done so if his Lord had referred personal disputes to the cognizance of an ecclesiastical council? No man will say so.

The ingenious Dr. Campbell, who, in his lectures on church history, has treated this subject with demonstrative clearness, alleges the acceptation of the word among the Jews with signal success.* He shows that it was appropriated with them in the same manner either to the whole nation or Church of Israel, which was a type of the universal Church of Christ, or to those that met for worship in the same synagogue. Now, this being the then received acceptation in the time of our Lord, he would not have been understood, had he employed it in any other; and as he could not intend the whole commonwealth of Christians, it must be a congregation of Christians. But how unintelligibly do they represent Christ as speaking, who give so many acceptations to the word church? Suppose we insert

---

* See Dr. Campbell's Lectures on Church History, vol. 1, p. 320.

congregation instead of church, who would understand him to refer to ecclesiastical courts. Yet *congregation* is no more fixed by Presbyterians to their assemblies for public worship, than εκκλησια was to denote the members of a synagogue, or of an apostolical church. Neither is εκκλησια more applicable, nor indeed is it so applicable to the various Presbyterian assemblies, as *congregation*. A synod or general assembly might have been at first denominated congregation, as well as by the term by which they are now known. What Presbyterian now would say "tell it to the congregation," intending by that a church court. Yet this would not be more senseless than what they attribute to the Lord Jesus Christ.

Another argument Dr. Campbell brings, equally convincing, is derived from the practice of the churches in the first ages. "Another collateral and corroborative evidence," says he, "that by εκκλησια is here meant not a representative body, but the whole of a particular congregation, is the actual usage of the church for the first three hundred years. I had occasion formerly to remark, that as far down as Cyprian's time, which was the middle of the third century, when the power of the people was on the decline, it continued to be the practice, that nothing in matters of scandal and censure could be concluded, without the consent and approval of the congregation. And this, as it appears to have been pretty uniform, and to have subsisted from the beginning, is, in my opinion, the best commentary which we, at this distance, can obtain on the passage." See page 325, vol. 1.

I may add farther, that the circumstance of the word *church* being afterwards used to signify the house of worship, is a very clear corroborative argument to show that an individual worshipping assembly of Christians, and not a representative body of church rulers, or the churches of a particular district, was first so called. Though this be not Scriptural, yet it shows the primitive application of the word, when the house received the name of the assembly. Just as the Jewish houses of worship were called synagogues, from the assembling of the people therein. This shows what sort of assembly a church was. Had it been a meeting of church rulers, like a Synod, &c., none but the places of their assembling would have been called *churches*. This, in my opinion, is the most unexceptionable species of historic proof. It can never be biased, and is often the surest criterion of the truth of facts.

CHAPTER VII.

THE INDEPENDENCY OF THE APOSTOLICAL CHURCHES PROVED FROM THE APOSTOLICAL INJUNCTIONS, AND INFERRED FROM OTHER CIRCUMSTANCES IN THE EPISTLES.

NOT only is the independency of individual churches proved from the origin, and profane and sacred acceptation of the word by which they are denominated; but the laws and regulations given by the apostles for their direction, put the matter beyond doubt. The whole discipline of Christ's house is, without exception, committed to the individual church, consisting of the pastors and brethren of one congregation. Apostolical injunctions, which cannot be obeyed in any other than an Independent church, implies the necessity of Independency. Now of this sort, are all the rules, with respect to the administration of discipline. It is the whole church, and not a church session, that is to receive members. Rom. xiv. 1.—" Him that is weak in the faith, *receive ye*."—" *Receive ye*." Now, no Presbyterian congregation could comply with this injunction. The brethren have nothing to do with the receiving of members. This province is entirely usurped by the minister and lay-elders. The epistle to the Corinthians, is addressed to the Church of God at Corinth, which is explained, 1 Cor. i. 2, to consist, not of minister and lay-elders, but of " them that are sanctified in Christ Jesus, called to be saints." Now, the power of excommunication is expressly vested in the whole church (chap. v. 4), not in church rulers alone. If a Presbyterian congregation would presume to interfere with their rulers upon such a point, it would be actual rebellion. Nay, the whole congregation, minister, elders, and people could not put away from their communion the grossest adulterer, if the superior ecclesiastical judicatories would think proper to skreen him. But the church at Corinth, is commanded to put away from *among themselves,* that wicked person (verse 13), and to purge out the old leaven (verse 7). To judge of the application of discipline, that is to examine and judge whether a crime be chargeable upon an accused member, is also stated (verse 12), to be the business of the whole church. " Do ye not judge them that are within ?" The whole church is to judge the accused person, though the church rulers are to execute the judgment. Now, a church which cannot admit an apostolical direction, cannot be apostolically constituted. Indeed, excommunication, though the highest act of church authority, is so peculiarly the business of the whole church, that the apostle does it not himself by an act of apostolical authority, but commits it to the saints themselves, that there might be an example and model to all future ages. Likewise, in Gal. v. 12, he does not say, " I cut off those that trouble you," but " I would that they were cut off." The restoration of fallen brethren upon repentance, is also the duty of the whole church, 2 Cor. ii. 6, 7, 8 ; Gal. vi. 1. Here, it is observable, that the excommunication was not the act of a select part of the church, but " was inflicted of many." We have also seen that the church was the final judge of personal and civil disputes among its members—Matt. xviii. 17 ; 1 Cor. vi. In these, and other instances, the instructions and commands given, necessarily suppose the constitution of the church to which they were directed, to have been Independent ; for to no other could they have been applied ; in no other could they have been executed.

It will not be deemed a sufficient answer to this, that the apostolical discipline may be executed in spirit and substance, though not by those apostolically appointed. The thing must not only be done, but done as it is commanded. The command must not only be obeyed in its primary object, but in the appointed manner, by the divinely appointed agents. Here we have not only the thing commanded to be done, but the persons commanded to do it. We may as well say, that we need not execute apostolical discipline, as that it may not be done by those apostolically appointed. The judges are here as clearly appointed, as the thing to be judged. To fulfil a law, we must not only do the thing the law directs, but in the manner directed by the law. The law ordains the murderer to die, but it does not warrant any but those legally appointed to judge, condemn, and execute him. The king summons his parliament; but the senators, intent upon their rural amusements, or the improvement of their estates, send their stewards. They meet; they enact laws; they send them to the king. Will he, will the constitution recognise such legislators? And will the Lord Christ recognise the proceedings of the unconstitutional judicatories, of what are called representative churches? Shall they be excused, who on account of business, amusement, or indolence have neglected their duty as church-members? They have no more authority to delegate the performance of this, than of any other duty which they owe to society, to their families, or to God. Would private Christians let any one persuade them, that they were to be present in heaven by representation only? It would be every whit as easy to prove the one as the other. In all the New Testament, there is not the shadow of a representation, in the Church of Christ.

To attend to the affairs of Christ's house, is the *privilege* of all church members. It argues ingratitude, contempt, and indifference, to transfer that right to others. But this is not only a privilege, but a duty, and each member is answerable for the personal discharge of it. Every individual member has the king's commission, and the king's command, to attend to the affairs of his kingdom, in concert with his brethren. If any neglect their duty, or pretend to depute others to represent them, they are guilty of disobedience to Christ, indifference to his laws, interest, and honour; and are traitors, as presuming to alter the constitution of his church. If any man, or body of men, assume the right by invasion, or accept it by delegation, they are usurpers, and act without, and contrary to the king's commands. But the very idea of a transference of duty, in religious matters, is absurd. None can think, judge, or act for another, with respect to spiritual things.

I have supposed the work to be done, and discipline to be duly administered. But I deny that this ever is, or can be the case in a perfect manner, when *they* do not the work who are divinely appointed. The imperfect state of discipline, in all Presbyterian churches, fully proves the assertion. Some of them, indeed, have a multiplicity of human rules, which they are very rigorous in putting into execution; but I know not any, that act fully up to the discipline of the churches of the New Testament.

Not only is discipline and all church power committed to the individual church, but every direction, command, and exhortation is suited to such alone. There are laws sufficient in the New Testament for the government and conducting of an Independent church, but not a single rule, or precept, or example for the government of a number of churches combined. All its rules and examples are applicable to individual congregations only. Independent churches have either precept or example for every case that can possibly occur. They are not obliged to proceed one step upon dubious ground. But it is evident that Presbyterians are obliged to vindicate their discipline, &c., by borrowing what is applied to individual churches. Thus the epistles to the church at Rome, to the church at Corinth, &c., &c., are epistles to individual churches, and speak uniformly either of individual duties, or reciprocal duties of church-members, and of the duties of the elders to the flock, and of the flock to the elders. But there is not a word as to the duties of elders as members of an ecclesiastical assembly, or of the duties of private Christians as members of an associated church. Now, if there was such a thing as an associated church under the same government, is it not strange we should have no rules with respect to it; that elders should have no directions as to their duties in these assemblies; and private Christians as to their relations to them? The individual flock is often called upon to obey their pastors or rulers, but never is either flock or shepherd commanded to obey a superior assembly. The apostles frequently and earnestly inculcate love among the church members, and warn them against schism and divisions. Not a word, however, do they say as to the duty of union among several churches under the same government, nor of the sin of one church separating from another. Is not this a plain proof that they were not externally joined? But men have got a convenient way of quoting Scripture now; for what is said (1 Cor. i. 10), against the members of the same individual church going into factions and parties, they apply to prove the sin of one church separating from another, or individuals separating from the church in which they were educated. We never hear the terrific word *schism* in any other sense in modern application. But it is evident that the schisms which the apostle here reprobates, are not the separation of a part even of an individual church, so as to form another; for this may be often done to advantage; it is the members of the same church running into factions and cabals, against which he speaks. Thus, in every other instance, they have to borrow what is spoken to individual churches, and apply it to associated churches. Either the Scriptures are lame, or such associations are unscriptural.

There are various other indirect hints in the epistles, which will occur to the reader who is accustomed *to mine* into the Word of God, and *weigh* each particle, as more precious than the gold of Ophir. Truth is ever consistent, and that opinion which does not gain strength from a progressive acquaintance with the Scripture, is not likely to be a Scripture truth. That hypothesis that forbids a minute attention to the most casual and indirect circumstance divinely recorded, cannot be well founded. An instance of what I mean, we have in 2 Cor. iii. 1. The apostle reasons that he had not, like others, need of recommendatory letters either to or *from the church* at Corinth. Now, the manner of the apostle's speaking here, would have been altogether improper, had the church at Corinth been under Presbyterian church government. He speaks of the recommendatory letters as necessary to some, but unnecessary to him, as coming from the *Church*, not the Presbytery. Had the apostle been a Presbyterian, he would have subjected himself and this church to severe censure, had he received credentials from it. This is the prerogative of the Presbytery or church rulers alone.* How would a modern church judicatory resent it, if a Probationer were to receive credentials from one of their congregations? The apostle himself could not be received into the General Synod, if he could not produce his credentials from his Presbytery. Nor could any minister or congregation *regularly* give him their pulpit.

The whole strain of the letters of the apostle Paul to the churches, shows them to have been Independent. He uniformly addresses, praises, or blames the church itself, and never a church session or ecclesiastical council of any sort. In chapters v. and xi. of 1 Cor. he blames the whole members, with respect to the incestuous person, and their irregularities in eating the Lord's Supper. Had they been under Presbyterian government, the *brethren* could not have been guilty, in keeping the fornicator, because they had no authority for putting him out. The session and superior courts would have been exclusively to blame; and would, undoubtedly, have received marked apostolical censure. If improper persons are admitted to communion among Presbyterians, what private member takes the guilt upon himself; but, if he disapproves of it, exclaims against the session. Upon the same persons should the abuses of the Lord's Supper have been principally chargeable.

In like manner, when our Lord writes to the seven churches of Asia, he praises or blames them individually. He never censures one, for the errors of another, though, with great severity, he reprimands each, for the errors of any part of itself. He charges the whole church as guilty, in keeping or retaining in communion an erroneous or profligate member; but he

---

* See also Acts xviii. 27. When Apollos was disposed to pass over into Achaia, he received recommendatory letters from the brethren, not a classical Presbytery.

never charges one church, with the errors of another. Now, if they had been under the Presbyterian form of church government, all the churches would have been chargeable with the faults and defects of each, as much as the whole individual church was chargeable with those of its members. Neither does he call upon the one to reform the other; but each to reform itself. Now, had the churches of Lesser Asia been Presbyterian, our Lord would have written to the Synod or Presbytery, and not to the individual churches to reform themselves. A Presbyterian congregation cannot reform itself. Christ, therefore, could not have been the author of Presbytery.

CHAPTER VIII.

OBJECTIONS ANSWERED.

Having investigated the claims of Presbytery and Independency upon Scripture evidence, it may be proper to take notice of some objections that I have heard urged against the scheme which I defend. Some of these are really so futile, that I am almost ashamed to bring them forward, to give them a formal refutation. But I have observed in conversation on this subject, that when the advocates of Presbytery are driven from the Scriptures, they sometimes shelter themselves under the supposed defects of Independency, or advantages of Presbytery. And it is really astonishing with what superficial reasoning, they will impose upon themselves. A few of such objections I will mention, and dispatch with the utmost brevity.

1. It is alleged that "there are too many sects already, and that we should rather endeavour to unite those that are already formed, than form another." I perfectly agree with the objector, that there are too many sects already, and that it is our duty to endeavour to unite Christians in all things. But how is this to be done? Is it by each party proposing to throw away a part of what they look upon to be truth, and embrace a little of what they consider wrong, that they may splice up a worldly union? Is it by the church rulers of different sects, meeting to compromise their differences, like a reference after a quarrel in a country fair? Is it by such language as this, "I will give up so much, give you up so much, and we will meet?" Is this a Scriptural way to unite sects? Is it not rather for each to appeal to the Bible, and meet on that common ground? Should not the language be, "we cannot all be right, let us then try our systems by the standard of truth, adopt whatever it recommends,

and reject whatever it condemns?" Truly it is a very modest way of reasoning, that there are so many sects already, that there is no room for introducing the model which Christ hath left us in the churches of the apostles! If once Christians could be brought to *feel* it their duty to *cease from man*, and renounce every standard but the Bible, they would not be long in uniting. Every union that is attempted, or effected upon other grounds, is not of God, but of the world.

2. It is suspected that "the encouragement that is given to call in question the opinions of our forefathers, and scrutinize them so severely by the Scriptures, will excite such a spirit of innovation, that it will lead to universal scepticism." Nay, some go so far as actually to fix the time when such inquirers must be advanced into atheists.

Truly it is a very astonishing thing that a habit of searching the Word of God, of relying implicitly upon it, and comparing all human opinions with that standard, must lead to scepticism. As well may it be said, that a habit of trusting God will lead us to distrust him. The Scriptures then are to blame for commending the Bereans for "searching the Scriptures daily whether these things were so." If our ancestors at the Reformation, had been afraid of these consequences, they never would have dared to call in question the ancient usages of their fathers, or to have condemned them by the Word of God. Never can any hurt arise from searching the Scriptures, and a habit of being regulated by them. "To the law and to the testimony, if they speak not agreeable to this Word, it is because there is no light in them."

I do not however mean to say, that there are no extremes on this side of the question; but I do say, that these do not consist in comparing every human opinion about divine things, with the Word of God; in rejecting every tittle of what is contrary to this standard; and adopting the merest minutiæ of what is pointed out. To run into extremes here, must be to go farther than the Scriptures. While we keep upon this ground, we cannot advance too far. But in searching the Scriptures upon this, as well as every other subject, there is great need of humility, and a consciousness of our own nothingness in the sight of God. If ever we begin the search with a desire to go beyond others, and have the honour to be more sharp sighted than those who preceded us, we shall certainly err. The natural pride of the human heart shows itself in various ways, and it is not strange that it should sometimes lead even good men into singularities. The Scriptures are plain, but it is only "the Spirit that can lead us into all truth." In searching the Scriptures for the mind of God, we should never neglect to ask, not formally, but earnestly and continually, the guidance of that heavenly conductor. O what prayer! what self-abasement! what a thirst for truth! what self-denial, are necessary in those who would advance in the knowledge of divine things! If we depend upon our own superior sagacity, if we prize not the smallest Scripture truth as more precious than rubies, and are not ready to give up the dearest earthly possessions and connections rather than part with it; if we have not simplicity of view, and a single eye to the glory of God, it will not be strange if we go astray in our search. But if we are made willing to receive truth at the greatest risk, and conscious of our weakness, incessantly and importunately to crave the direction of the Spirit, I do not think that the God of truth will suffer us to be led astray. Whilst, therefore, we, like the Bereans, search the Scriptures for ourselves, let us not be *heady* or *high-minded*, but humbly wait at the feet of Jesus, to learn wisdom from his lips.

3. It is alleged that "the Presbyterian form of government is better calculated to repress heresy, preserve purity of doctrine, and authoritatively settle all disputes that arise among their congregations." But I ask how have they this power? Is it by force or persuasion? If it is by the latter, then Independents enjoy it in its utmost latitude; if it is by the former, then the Gospel disclaims it; Christ abhors it. Is not this evidently inconsistent with the whole spirit and letter of the Gospel? These are carnal, not spiritual weapons. Is not this to put a hand to the ark, and a distrust of the power of the Great Head of the Church, who bears it

upon his own shoulders? What is the crime in the nations which God hath always punished with the greatest rigour? Is it not that of presuming to take upon themselves the defence and protection of his people the Jews? Those who injured his people, are indeed punished; but those who stepped in between him and them, to take their confidence off himself, are punished with the utmost severity. Egypt, that oppressed Israel, was punished; but the crime was, as it were, afterwards forgotten; but Egypt that became the staff of Israel is not pardoned till this very day. From the overthrow of Nectanebus by Ochus, 350 years before Christ, it never has had a king of its own. Degraded from among the nations, governed by foreigners, enslaved and oppressed, God hath exhibited it as a malefactor in the gibbet, for a warning to others. He is as jealous of the prerogative of supporting his Church, as a husband is of the confidence and affection of his wife, and views every foreign interference, as an attack upon his honour. Will men, then, never learn to trust God with his own cause, and use only the means that he hath appointed to preserve his truths? Will they never cease to provoke his jealousy, by associations to defend his church? Is there any fear that ever the gates of hell will shake it off Immanuel's shoulders? Alas! that ever Christians should have thought of substituting human bulwarks, for the continual presence of Jehovah, who is as a *wall of fire around his Zion!*

But the Presbyterian method of preserving orthodoxy, and settling disputes, is not only unscriptural, but is always without any real advantage. They may keep their members from preaching contrary to their standard, but can they enable " the blind to lead the blind, without both falling into the ditch." Force may make a hypocrite, but can never make a Christian. Interest may constrain a carnal man to profess the leading truths of the Gospel, but midnight darkness will reign in his congregation. Among many there is a continual cry of *soundness* and *orthodoxy*, who appear to every spiritual man to be destitute of the truth, as it is in Jesus, and to hold the truth in unrighteousness.

Even among the stricter sects of Presbyterians, I am constrained to say, that while some of them do not fail to show their zeal by lifting up a testimony against the corruptions of the General Synod, they appear to be *hunting* after the world with equal avidity. And I know where it is said, "If any man love the world, the love of the father is not in him."

4. It is alleged in behalf of Presbytery that "in the multitude of counsellors there is safety; that several congregations must have more wisdom than one; and that an assembly of learned men must be better qualified to transact church matters than an ignorant multitude."

This reasoning might have some effect, if there was any thing left to the wisdom of man. The generality of Christians, are the "weak things of this world," and of all men living they are the least qualified for the arduous duty of legislation. But thanks be to God, he hath left no such things to be done by any. Every necessary law and direction are given, and nothing more is necessary, than to judge of their application, to which the most ordinary capacity is equal, in the use of the appointed means, and under the promised guidance of the Spirit. Poor despised Christians would indeed be ill qualified to appear in what is impiously styled a court of Christ. But the meanest and most ignorant of them are equal to judge of every case of discipline, that can occur in Christ's house; for it is said that "they shall be all taught of God." And indeed I would expect a more just determination from such, than from the representatives of all the churches on earth. Christ's presence is with the one, as being according to his own appointment, while it is likely the other shall be left to their own wisdom.*

---

* Such objectors differ very widely from the Apostle Paul, who supposes that even the weakest saints are capable of judging not merely of the spiritual concerns of the church, but also of settling the civil disputes of the brethren. 1. Cor. vi. 4.—"If then ye have judgments of things pertaining to this life, set them to judge who are least esteemed in the church." We are not to suppose from this however, that a church is always to select "the least esteemed" for the arbitration of civil differ-

I have heard, that the most usual, and the most effectual way that certain persons have taken to prejudice the minds of the people of this country against Independents, is, by representing them as "disorderly;"—"without discipline;"—"breaking down the hedge;"—"not coming in by the door."

In the New Testament, Christ calls himself the door; if any one, then, come not in at this door, I

ences. In my opinion the spirit of the passage is this—differences among brethren should be settled by arbitration of the church. Some of the Corinthians had transgressed this rule, and shown, by their appealing to the civil law, that they supposed there were not any among their brethren fit for this office. The apostle takes fire at the supposition, that those who were to judge wicked men and angels as assessors with Christ in the great day, should be esteemed unfit to judge in such comparatively trivial matters; and to show them that he looked upon all Christians to be qualified for this business, he bids them choose from among themselves even those that were accounted the weakest. As if he had said, to show you that they are wise in whom the Spirit of God dwells, let the "least esteemed" brethren be singled out upon any emergency, and they will wisely determine the matter. Then he subjoins, "I speak this to your shame;" you have looked upon all your brethren as unwise or unjust; the Spirit of God declares them all, even the least esteemed of them to be qualified to settle your disputes. Are you not then ashamed of your opinion and conduct, with respect to your brethren, judging so unfavourably of them, and differing so much from the judgment of God? That the apostle looked upon all the saints as fit for such an office, is clear, not only from the words "least esteemed," but also from the arguments of illustration in the 2nd and 3rd verses.—The saints judging the world and fallen angels. All the saints small and great, shall have this honour; therefore, to make the argument conclusive, all the saints must be fit for the duty of arbitration. But that a church is not bound *always* to select the "least esteemed" for this purpose, is clear, not only from the spirit of the passage already explained, but from what follows in the 5th verse—"Is it so that there is not a wise man amongst you? No, not one that shall be able to judge between his brethren?" This question supposes, that the church was at liberty to choose the wisest among the brethren. If then, the "least esteemed," are qualified judges, they are inexcusable, who will not be amenable to the decision of the most esteemed in the church: Corollary: If the weakest brethren are qualified to decide in matters of property, without appealing to the superior learning, wisdom, or judicial knowledge of a Presbytery or Synod, nay, without even appealing to the civil law, much more are they qualified to judge of every thing, as to the discipline of Christ's house.

heartily consent that all pulpit doors be shut against him. God is said to have made a hedge about his vineyard. But it seems now, that not Christ, but the Presbytery is *the door*, and, that the hedge of God's laws and institutions is not sufficiently high and prickly to keep out wild beasts, but it must be new-made, or at least mended by synodical authority. I am afraid that the generality, even of Christians, in this country, are much mistaken in their notions of the discipline of Christ's house. It is not the punctual attention to a wide system of human rules and regulations, that deserves the name of discipline, but the faithful execution of all the laws, given by Christ in the New Testament. Those sects, who, in this country, are most highly applauded for discipline, have, indeed, a rigorous code of human laws, and are peculiarly strict in the observance of them; but this is not discipline, but ecclesiastical usurpation and tyranny. Christ's discipline is calculated to prevent the entrance of the carnal professor, or to discover him, if he has been admitted. But, such a person, if he has a decent behaviour, and a sound of orthodoxy, might pass his life in the most rigorous Presbyterian connections, without detection. He must, indeed, have a considerable portion of pharisaical righteousness, but he will be admitted and continued without the life and power of godliness. This is a bold charge; if any sect of Presbyterians think it unjust, let them repel it. Before they can do this, they must be able to declare, that there is not an individual in their connection, that they do not look upon as a member of Christ. If they cannot make this declaration, their discipline is defective. I can refer them to an Independent church, consisting of more than six hundred members, in which, each individual can make this declaration concerning his brethren. I am therefore constrained to charge such objectors either with the grossest ignorance, or wilful misrepresentation. A want of discipline is what I charge upon Presbyterians. This is among the chief objections I have to them. "By their traditions, they have made void the law of God." But let them produce one single rule of discipline, appointed by Christ, which Independents refuse to admit. If they can show them any thing in Scripture, which they have not hitherto observed, I am sure they will not act up to their principles, if they do not adopt it with gratitude. But if they must be called "disorderly," because they reject the interference of man, in the things of God, because they refuse obedience to any rules but those of Christ, they are not concerned to repel the charge.

6. When Presbyterians are driven from the Bible, they sometimes shelter themselves under the wings of learned and pious men. "Are you wiser or better than our ancestors, who have shed their blood for Presbytery? If ever the spirit of God was with any body of men, it was with the Westminster divines." With some, it is very common to point at the Reformation as perfect, and every declension in principle or practice in professors, is a declension, not from the Scriptures, but the *Reformation.* They must indeed be blind, who do not look upon the Reformation as the greatest national blessing any people ever experienced; but those who thus idolize the Reformers, are guilty of setting up another God in Israel. However much we have been benefited by their labours, however, eminent were their attainments, it is "to the law, and to the testimony," not to the Reformers, we are directed as the standard of truth. As to the Westminster assembly, I am neither concerned to accuse nor condemn them. Episcopacy, Presbytery, and Independency have each had some of the most pious men in the list of their defenders; the Christian then can have no safe guide but the Bible.

CHAPTER IX.

REASONS WHY SOME ARE APT TO CONCLUDE, THAT THERE IS NO CHURCH MODEL IN SCRIPTURE.

I HAVE now given my reasons, why it is probable that the Scriptures of the New Testament contain a model of church government, and have examined the pretensions of Presbytery and Independency. Before I dismiss the subject of church government, I think it not amiss, to point out a few reasons, why some ingenious and pious men have not been able to discover any definite plan of any kind. If disinterested enquirers differ materially upon any point, in the examination of which they draw from a common source, there is likely to be some circumstances in their situation which leads to the difference: something that tends to involve the subject of inquiry.

1. In my opinion, one thing that tends to prevent some from seeing a model of church government in the New Testament, is, their being accustomed to take their ideas of the government of a spiritual, from that of temporal kingdom. They are apt to expect a vigorous plan, a-kin to their ideas of the best constituted civil governments. Whatever they judge the best calculated to govern a kingdom of this world, they look upon to be the fittest for the kingdom of Christ. In examining the Scriptures, then, it is no wonder they pass and repass the apostolical model, without seeing it. This is too simple to be effectual. Like Naaman the Syrian, who thought he was mocked by the prophet, when he prescribed as his cure, to wash in the waters of Jordan, they do not think it worth their trouble, even to give it a trial. They must have a firm and coercive plan, calculated to sustain christianity, and avenge it of its adversaries, as civil

rights are by civil laws. In this view I grant that the apostolical government must disappear, when brought into contrast or competition with either Presbytery or Episcopacy. Presbytery is a vigorous republic; but as I said elsewhere, *this* is not calculated to govern a single carnal family. It would be totally inefficient in worldly policy. To those, then, who have these worldly ideas, of Christ's kingdom, Independency is like David going out with his sling and pebbles against Goliah.

2. Others are much influenced by the carnal institutions, and pompous and multifarious Jewish heirarchy and sanhedrim. They are apt to transfer their ideas of the government of the Jewish church, to that of the Christian. If they are too impartial and enlightened to pretend to see any thing of this nature in the New Testament, they are inclined to think, that for this reason, we are left to form a model of church government for ourselves, according to time and circumstances. They do not find what they expect, and they hastily conclude that nothing is to be found.

3. Many inquirers have been all their lives so accustomed to the pompous, multifarious, and complicated systems of Presbytery, and Episcopacy, that when they go to the New Testament, they are led to overlook the simple apostolical plan. Their minds are filled with these intricate and punctilious systems, and are so habituated to the voluminous canons, laws, rules, regulations, acts, &c., &c., &c., which are to be found in almost all modern churches, that the Scripture directions for church government, appear altogether defective, obscure, and inadequate. They look into the Scriptures —they can find neither the Church of England, nor the Church of Scotland, nor any of the numerous sects formed on the same model—they instantly conclude, that there is no form of government revealed, or at most, is only coarsely blocked, to be variously formed or shaped according to the different humours of succeeding ages.

4. Another reason why some are inclined to conclude that there is nothing delivered in Scripture sufficient for the government of a church, is, that many writers have represented the matter much more clear, full, and

G

express, than it is in reality. With some there is not a doctrine more clearly and fully revealed in Scripture. They can see their favourite system in almost every page. When we hear men arguing from the tabernacle of Moses, to the polity of the Christian church, and asserting that Christ's faithfulness engaged him to be as explicit, full, and particular in giving a model for the government of his church, as Moses was in erecting the tabernacle, and thus determining *a priori*, with the most arrogant confidence, what Christ must have done, instead of considering what he has actually done, we are apt to expect *the most stately fabric*. When we go to the Scriptures themselves, if we cannot see through the magnifying glasses of particular sects, and swallow their *high probabilities* for demonstration, we are ready to conclude that there is no definite model at all. They make us expect a giant; we see a man of nothing but the ordinary size; and from our disappointment, we are ready to look upon him as a very dwarf. When we are made to expect too much, we are apt to be chagrined with our disappointment; and from our previous high imagination, we think the object more insignificant than it really is. Dr. Pococke tells us he had formed such an idea of the celebrated cataracts of the Nile, from the exaggerated accounts of former travellers, that when he came in sight of them, so very much did they fall below his expectations, so far from thinking these to be the objects of his curiosity, he asked when he should reach them; and it was not without surprise, that he was told they were already in view. Such is the case with many when they go to look for church government in the Scriptures.

5. Another thing that tends to hide the Scripture model from some inquirers, is their expectation of a *systematic* plan, or a formal treatise on the subject. They look for a *jointed* scheme, as methodically detailed, as Presbytery is exhibited in the Westminster Confession. When they look into the New Testament for such a plan, there is nothing like it to be found; the half of the whole epistles would scarcely contain such a system. The conclusion, then, is, that no form of church government is revealed. I would ask such

inquirers, upon what do they found their expectation of a system, or formal treatise on church government? Is there in the whole range of revelation, anything like a system, upon any subject? Is there any doctrine, is there any precept in Scripture delivered systematically? Take, for instance, the doctrine of the atonement; we do not find all the texts that illustrate this doctrine, collected into a system, but scattered from the beginning to the end of revelation. In the same manner, doctrines and precepts are not kept distinct, but intentionally intermingled, as it were, to prevent daring men from separating them, and setting up the one in opposition to the other. Doctrines are there taught practically, and precepts as flowing from the doctrines. We have in the same reasoning, in the same period, doctrine and precept. Thus in Phil. ii. 5–11, we have the doctrine of Christ's equality with the Father, and the precept of humility, as flowing from this, in the same period.

Indeed the manner of the revelation of divine truth, seems everywhere calculated and intended to excite to industry and search, and overcome our natural love of ease. Nothing is got by the lazy and inattentive. While on the one hand the great truths of revelation are so plain, that a man may, as it were, "run and read," being found in every page, so that "the wayfaring man, though a fool, cannot err therein;" on the other, it is so wisely regulated to spur us to exertion, that to exhibit completely, in all its features and bearings, and effectually prove any one point, it is necessary to turn over and over, search every page, compare spiritual things with spiritual, and examine the same doctrine in the different connections and views in which it is found in Scripture. In one text a doctrine is taught, perhaps with all its essential parts, but with some of its features more marked and prominent than others, according to the purpose the Holy Spirit meant it to serve on that particular occasion. In another, the same truth is brought forward in a different point of view, to serve a different purpose, with the features that were less prominent in the other, now more marked and distinct. Like a painter who would exhibit the same scene in a multiplicity of views, alternately bringing forward and putting into the background the different objects which he wants to represent. In one representation we have a palace as the chief object of attention, and its owner and family walking at some distance, are seen indistinctly. In another, the owner, if a celebrated personage, is represented as the chief object, and the palace is put into the shade. In another, if the painter has an intention to show us principally, some surprising and romantic scenery, we will see the palace and the master both put into the back-ground. Now, that we may form a clear and distinct notion of the master, the palace, and the scenery, we must view all the three pictures alternately, though all are represented in every one of them. Just so it is in Scripture. Its truths are so scattered, and variously represented, upon such various occasions, for so many distinct purposes, that we cannot have a complete view of any one of them, without examining the whole Bible. They are so interwoven, and have such a connection and mutual dependence upon each other, that a knowledge of one truth cannot thoroughly be obtained without a pretty general acquaintance with all the rest.* How absurd is it, then, to expect a system or formal treatise on church government! If the greatest truths of Scripture are revealed in this manner, how unreasonable is it to expect a different method on this point! Yet it appears to me that an attentive observer will find that the reason why many conclude there is no form of church government laid down in Scripture, is, because they do not find *a system.*

6. Some are led to think that there is no complete model intended to be exhibited in the New Testament, because all we have on this subject is given indirectly, and as it were unintentionally, and not sufficiently and fully explained. I have already hinted at the reason why the subject could not be consistently handled in

---

* I am sure I have found the advantage of this mode of revelation in examining this subject. Had it been methodically laid down in one place, and been accompanied with no difficulties, I would have been deprived of much additional knowledge, which I obtained, on many points, in my search.

an express and copious manner. As we are nowhere known in Scripture, but in the person of the first churches, we could not expect a direct address on the subject of church government: what is said to them is said to us. And as it would be absurd to expect that an apostle, after *forming a church* in any place, would, in a subsequent letter, give them express directions for *the formation of a church*, seeing this was already done; all we can expect is an indirect, and as it were, an unintentional allusion to what was done, and a scattered picture of their church order. Instead, then, of being disappointed at this mode of communication, no other can we reasonably expect. Indirect hints, incidental observations, and a passing view of their practice, is all that the *manner* of revelation can admit. The knowledge of their church order must necessarily be obtained from passages where the apostles are professedly treating of something else. But this is not the only thing to be proved in this manner. The chief knowledge that we have upon many other points, is obtained exactly in this indirect and circuitous way. A distinction between ordinary and extraordinary officers is generally admitted; yet the exact boundaries of their office is nowhere professedly and directly treated. A standing ministry is generally granted, yet the chief proofs of this must be obtained from incidental, indirect, and as it were, unintentional hints, and the example of the apostolical churches. To prove the truth of the Scriptures themselves, or any of their doctrines, nothing more is necessary than sufficient evidence to convince the humble earnest inquirer. It is by no means necessary to silence the caviller, and divest the disobedient of every pretext. There is not a single doctrine of revelation, the investigation and proof of which, is not accompanied with difficulties. "There must be heresies, that they which are approved may be made manifest." If, then, there are difficulties, even with respect to truths necessary to salvation, is it strange that there should be more in matters of comparatively less importance?

But though the subject is not largely explained and directly inculcated, the scattered incidental hints we have, when united, will be found not at all deficient for the purposes of church government. They will be found so complete, that a church of Christ will not be obliged to advance a step but on sacred ground. If this be the case, I would ask, what more do people want? I acknowledge that this mode of conveying divine truth does not suit those who inquire under the influence of a worldly spirit. When this is the case, it will not be strange if the Scripture materials should appear extremely scanty, and obscure, or confused. He will be too ready to think himself justifiable to take the side of worldly interest, unless the glare of evidence be such that it is impossible to resist it. He must be driven to duty by the thunders of Sinai, and not constrained by the gentle voice of Christ, when he says, "He that loveth me, keepeth my commandments." But we should not ask, like Henry IV. of France, "Is there salvation in such a church?" but with the apostle, "Lord what would'st thou have me to do?" ready to perform the least, as well as the greatest, of his commandments. We should continually hang upon the lips of our Master, ready with the alacrity and alertness of an angel, to perform his pleasure, glad of discovering it, though it should rob us of our property, or even our life. Such inquirers, I apprehend, will, after leisurely investigation, have no need to complain of a want of Scripture materials on this subject.

CHAPTER X.

CHARACTER OF CHURCH MEMBERS—OR THE NECESSITY OF PURE COMMUNION.

I HAVE now stated my views of church government, which, after an impartial and leisurely search, I have been constrained to embrace. But I have other reasons for separating from the General Synod, which still more pungently touch my conscience. One of these is the continual necessity I would be under, of prostituting the ordinances of Christ, by promiscuous communion. I shall therefore devote this chapter to point out the character of the members of the apostolical churches, and prove the necessity of pure communion. If I succeed, it will be evident, that I cannot conscientiously remain in a connection in which I am obliged to transgress so important a law of Christ. Even were I still a friend to Presbyterian government, I could not hold communion with the General Synod, nor any other Presbyterian connection that I am acquainted with. In none of them that I know of, is there purity of communion. Many of them, indeed, have raised very high human hedges around the Lord's table, and have enjoined very rigid terms of communion; but in none of them, I believe, is *credible evidence of the new birth* the test of membership. The gate is indeed shut against the openly profane, but the *decent* worldling may pass. At the same time, the child of God is excluded, if he cannot digest all the peculiarities of the sect, and load his soul with a mass of human obligations. If I am mistaken with respect to any involved in this charge, I will be glad to retract my censure, upon convincing information. I do not write to compliment, neither do I write to expose, but to reform. This is a point which I know many Presbyterians will not dispute. They acknowledge its desirableness, but doubt in the present state of the church, as they speak, its practicability. Nay, all who exclude any, virtually acknowledge this principle. For if they exclude one sort of sinners, by what authority do they admit another? I beg, therefore, that Presbyterians of this description, will accompany me through this chapter. Though they are able to disprove all I have said on the subject of church government, yet if I can convince them, of the sinfulness of admitting to communion, any but the credible disciples of Christ, and to persuade them to act up to their convictions, I will not have lost my labour. I would be glad, indeed, to see any of the Presbyterian connections, even thus far reformed. I acknowledge, I have been guilty in this instance hitherto, and am persuaded, that nothing has contributed so much to render my labours so unfruitful, though I had not the same views of the subject which I have at present. I look upon promiscuous communion to resemble adultery —it must be viewed by a jealous God, with the utmost displeasure. What is the reason, while there are multiplied sects of flamingly orthodox Presbyterians, that darkness covers our land, and gross darkness the people? Is the fault in man or in God? "Behold the arm of the Lord is not shortened, that he cannot save, nor his ear heavy, that he cannot hear," &c.

When we look into the epistles for the character of the members of apostolical churches, we find that they were considered as members of the body of Christ, 1 Cor. i. 2. In writing to the church at Corinth the apostle denominates the members *sanctified in Christ Jesus, called to be saints.* Were I not already too voluminous, I would quote and illustrate the addresses and many other passages of the epistles to the churches, to show the character of the members of the apostolical churches; I must be contented with referring to them —Rom. i. 7; 2 Cor. i. 1; Eph. i. 1; Phil. i. 1; Col. i. 2; ii. 6; 1 Thes. i. 1; 2 Thes. i. 1; 1 Pet. i. 2; 2 Pet. i. 1; 1 Cor. vi. 11, 19, 20; x. 17; xii. 27; 2 Thes. ii. 13, 14; 1 Cor. x. 16, 17. These passages will clearly point out what is the character of those who ought to be recognized as church members. The church at Rome is commanded to receive him that is *weak in the faith*. Now, this supposes that they were in the habit of judging of those whom they admitted to membership, and that those who had *no faith* were not to be received. For if they deliberately received any without evidence of faith, there could be no propriety in commanding them to receive him that was *weak in faith*. "Give not that which is holy unto dogs," is as much a command of Christ, as "thou shalt not kill;" and whatever be its primary meaning, it is a general precept, and will hold more eminently true in this instance than in any other I am acquainted with. 1. Cor. iii. 10–16, is more naturally interpreted of the admission of church members, than of doctrines. Both the preceding and succeeding connection fix it to this. Christians, not doctrines, are the lively stones in God's building, and God's husbandry. His temple is to be built of these materials. It is not any doctrine, with respect to Christ, that is said to be the foundation; but he is the foundation *himself*. New members might be added to apostolical churches, but new doctrines could not be lawfully promulgated. In this sense, the apostles not only laid the foundation, but finished the house. There are neither gold, silver, nor precious stones now remaining to be built upon the foundation of the apostolical doctrines. But the gold, silver, and precious stones, beautifully represent converted church members, who are not injured by the fire, and their different degrees of value.* All are valuable; but while some are silver, others are gold, and other precious stones. On the other hand, unconverted church members are like wood, hay, and stubble, which will be consumed whenever fire is applied. The fire of temptation and persecution will try every church, during which, unconverted members will show their combustible nature, and be consumed. At least the fire of the great judgment will try the house of what sort of materials it is built, and the builders will either have loss or gain, according to the result of the trial.

---

* This interpretation is strengthened from Isaiah liv. 11–13, in which church members are represented under similar figures.

"And he himself shall be saved, yet so as by fire," with the utmost difficulty, as a man escaping from the midst of the flames. He being a servant of Christ himself, shall certainly have an entrance, but not an *abundant* entrance into heaven. Yea, and very probably, when the church is trying, by means of the fire of temptation and persecution, although he may be preserved from falling, he will be "saved by fire." Heavy trials and afflictions may be laid upon him, and the Lord may chastise him sore, though he may not give him over to death. He may be sorely scorched in the fire of affliction, although he be not burnt up. If this be the true interpretation of the passage, which is adopted by some of the best commentators, and which I have always thought the most natural, from the first time I heard it suggested, there is an awful lesson in it to every church ruler, and to every church member, not to hazard the peace and comfort of their own souls here, nor the loss of a part of their reward hereafter, by building God's house with combustible materials; admitting unconverted sinners to membership. But the character of church members is clearly determined from Acts ii. 47. "And the Lord added to the church daily such as should be saved," which is literally translated thus: "The Lord added the *saved* daily to the church." It does not mean that the Lord added to the church universal by conversion, though that is previously supposed; but that he added such as were converted to the church at Jerusalem. As soon as sinners are converted, they are *saved*, and none but the *saved* were added to the church at Jerusalem. It was the *Lord added them*, because the terms of admission were not the *prudential regulations* of the church, but the Scripture evidence of their being *saved*. The church was only God's instrument. "The Lord saved them," and the church seeing this, received them.

When we consider the character of the generality who sit down at the Lord's table, and then read that awful asseveration (1 Cor. xi. 27), it is enough to make the hand to tremble, which distributes among them the emblems of the body and blood of Christ. Indeed, I am really astonished that my conscience could ever have borne it. Ah! the guilt of professing Christians, in this single instance. If every unworthy communicant is a murderer, yea a murderer of the Lord Christ, what must be the guilt of all sects of Presbyterians? Is it any wonder that the labours of faithful individuals among them, should be in a great measure unproductive. If the murder of a man like ourselves be a crime so heinous, in the estimation of God and man, how aggravated a crime is the murder of the Son of God? What countless thousands of stupid sinners are permitted rashly to embrue their hands in the blood of Christ? Dreadful sentence! "Whosoever shall eat this bread, and drink this cup of the Lord unworthily, shall be guilty of the body and blood of the Lord." Now, how much more aggravated is the guilt of the church that admits such members, and the pastor that administers this ordinance to them? I know, indeed, that they usually hold themselves excused, by faithfully warning them of their dangers, and thus laying their blood upon their own heads. This indeed was my own refuge. I wished to persuade myself, that if I was faithful to point out the characters of such as were unworthy, in a clear and explicit manner, and fervently warn them of their danger, that then I was innocent. But I now clearly see that this refuge is untenable, and have plainly told my people, that I would no more administer that ordinance among them, in the same promiscuous manner, than I would descend from the pulpit with a sword in my hand to destroy them. I have no standard but the Bible, and am ready to change any erroneous sentiment or conduct, as soon as I discover it. We are frequently mistaken for want of having made any matter the subject of particular consideration. But if any minister of a feeling conscience, can allow himself, in the promiscuous administration of this ordinance, after his attention has been called to the subject, and having made it a matter of prayer and investigation, I am really astonished. The apology of faithfully warning will not stand even in human judgment, far less in the awful day of God. If I put a sword into the hand of an angry madman, it will be no excuse for me that I have warned him not to kill the person against whom he is enraged. I might have known he would not have listened to my counsel. So, if I put the emblems of Christ's body and blood into the hands of impenitent sinners, I may warn and warn, they are mad, and will not take warning, but rush upon their ruin. Suppose there is a madman standing in an apothecary's shop, while the apothecary is mixing up a dose of poison in a liquor of which the madman is very fond—the madman asks for a drink of it—the apothecary tells him there is poison in it—and that it will surely kill him if he drink it—the madman insists to have it, alleging that there is no fear, and that he can drink it without any injury—the apothecary still asserts that it will kill him if he will drink it; but if he persists in desiring to have it, he will give it him, rather than disoblige him—the madman reaches for it—the apothecary gives it, taking the madman and those present, and God himself to witness, that he is clear of his blood, for he hath faithfully warned him—the madman drinks—and dies. Reader, were you one of the jury to try the apothecary, would you clear him? Will the Lord clear him in his judgment? And in what does the apothecary differ from the pastor, who puts the emblems of Christ's body and blood into the hands of impenitent sinners? In nothing but in the degree of their guilt. The latter is the more guilty, inasmuch as the shedding of the blood of Christ is a greater crime than the shedding of the blood of a mere man; and inasmuch as the murder of a soul is a greater crime, than the murder of the body. It is no excuse, that great as the crime of unworthy partaking of the Lord's supper is, it is nevertheless pardonable. This is altogether with God, whether he will grant pardon and repentance or not; and although the individual is afterwards pardoned, the pastor's crime is not thereby mitigated. I have applied it particularly to the pastor, but every church member is guilty, and will be accountable; for it is not to one or a few, but to the whole church, that Christ has committed the discipline of his house.

I believe that *debarring* or *fencing the tables*, and *giving of tokens*, like all other human expedients in religion, have been of the most serious injury.* It is a bungling expedient to supply the want of Scripture discipline, and an apostolically constituted church. If none but those who are credibly Christians, were admitted to church membership, what occasion would there be for tokens of admission, or debarring. They will take their seats around Christ's table, as naturally as children will seat themselves unasked around the table of their earthly father. Who dare debar any such? And who dare invite any other? The custom of debarring, under the appearance of excluding the unworthy, is, in reality, only a pretext for admitting worldly men, without seeming to share in their guilt. Church rulers dare not professedly admit unregenerate men, from fear of offending God, and they dare not candidly deny them admission, from fear of men. They have, therefore, found out a way to compromise the matter between God and the world, by *fencing the tables*. Thus, they avoid giving individual offence, and driving unregenerate men away from their society, and imagine themselves clear as to the crimes of prostituting the ordinance of Christ. I ask, was ever this means found effectual to preserve purity of communion? I am sure I have tried it in the most awful manner in my power, and I do not know that it was in any degree effectual. Often, very often the hardened unawakened sinner, will let all pass through his ear as the

---

* Every one who receives a token, has the solemn declaration of church rulers, that they consider them as real Christians. For if it is granted that none but real Christians have a right to this ordinance, of what is this a token, if not of their fitness, at least in the estimation of those from whom they receive it? Now, if church rulers give a token to any whom they do not upon good evidence consider to be Christians, they are guilty of the most awful deceiving of sinners that can be imagined. They lead them, with a blind upon their eyes, to the brink of a precipice, and tell them, as they are falling, that they are tumbling into perdition. I beseech those Christians, who are engaged in this murderous business, to stop and reflect; to weigh this with seriousness and prayer. I believe that there are many who give tokens with a trembling heart, and a smiting conscience. Let them beware lest conscience, by the repetition of guilt, become callous and seared. Their state is awful, if it has ceased to smite.

path of an arrow through the air, while the weak and timid Christian will take what is said as against himself, and be discouraged. Indeed, they know very little of the human heart, who think that an unawakened sinner will take such a warning. I have laboured several hours with individuals, without convincing them of their danger. Till the Lord open the eyes of their understanding, they will still have some refuge of lies. How then could it be expected to prevail with a multitude, in a few minutes speaking, before the administration of the supper? I demand that those who practice it, will produce me either precept or example, either expressed or implied, for debarring and tokens of admission at the Lord's supper. If this cannot be produced, I argue that that church, which cannot maintain apostolical purity, without human expedients, is not apostolically constituted. When I see a wall supported by a buttress, I judge it has not a good foundation. When I see a human invention employed to prop an ordinance of Christ, I form a similar judgment.

But not only is the necessity of pure communion proved from the character of the members of the apostolical churches, and direct Scripture precept—the very model of the apostolical churches could not be otherwise preserved. Christ's laws are not at all calculated to govern the devil's subjects. Spiritual laws will take no hold of carnal men. If there are unregenerate members admitted and retained, they will throw all into confusion. They will stop the equability of the church's motion, and whenever the fire of temptation begins to burn, the house will fall with a crash in the midst of the flames. If they are not excluded, a majority must instantly be substituted for unanimity; human laws and human sanctions must be substituted for those of the New Testament. From one step to another, they will arrive to a full grown antichrist, and the more heads he will have, the more monstrous will he be.

I may add, there are ordinances of Christ which cannot be attended to, if strict purity of communion is not preserved. 1 Cor. vii. 1. That civil disputes should be determined by the church, is an apostolical ordinance, for the neglect of which, the Corinthians are severely reproved. But this is an ordinance which no church can ever observe, if they admit unregenerate men to membership. Such persons will yield to the decision of the church, if it be in their favour; but if it be against them, they will show little respect to the determination. Neither does the apostle's reasoning hold good with respect to such as judge, for *they* will not "*judge the world.*" Something like this, may, in smaller matters, be attempted in a mixed communion, among a few individuals, generally poor, and not able to maintain law-suits, having little civil intercourse; but can never effectually take place in all cases, except purity of communion be strictly adhered to.

Mutual exhortation in church meetings,* is another apostolical ordinance, 1 Cor. xiv. 29 ; 1 Thes. v. 11. Let any Presbyterian congregation give this liberty to private individuals, and they will soon see the house in flames. The wood, the hay, and the stubble, would instantly take fire, and it would be altogether impossible to preserve any sort of order or decorum. This would shiver them, as a cedar in Lebanon is splintered by the lightning. None but the children of Christ could bear or improve such a privilege. Now, that church which cannot bear an apostolical institution, is not apostolically constituted.

* As hypocrites will occasionally find admittance into the churches of Christ, such ordinances as these, seem wisely calculated to detect them. That which appears to worldly churches the most exceptionable in these ordinances, is, in reality, their great perfection, and prove their heavenly birth. They afford an expeditious way to discover, and exclude carnal professors. They are useful also to discipline the true soldiers of Jesus; they grind off their asperities, accustom them to forbearance, exercise their patience, and improve all their graces.

CHAPTER XI.

OBJECTIONS ANSWERED.

Many who look upon purity of communion, as a desirable thing, and go a certain length in effecting it, do not aim at a strict separation, apprehending the attempt to be either fruitless or dangerous. Some go so far as to shield themselves under Scripture example: I was once of this number myself. I shall therefore employ this chapter in answering the objections usually alleged against any attempt to effect a pure church.

Objection 1.—It is said, "we cannot know men's hearts; if they are sober and decent in their external conduct, and acknowledge their belief of the orthodox doctrines, we can go no farther."

This objection, if there was anything in it, would go to show that Christ has given a command to the churches, which it would not be in their power to put into practice. If Christ has said, "give not that which is holy unto dogs," he supposes we are able to distinguish the persons whom he intends, otherwise his advice is unimportant. A physician cannot look into the inner part of the human body, to see what is the disease of his patient, yet he judges of this, by the symptoms and appearances he beholds. Just so are we to judge of the human heart. If the fountain be salt, so will the streams; if the streams are fresh, we may judge that the fountain has also been made fresh. Our Lord tells us that a tree is known by its fruits. If there is faith in the heart, there will be obedience in the life. If there be spiritual life, there will be some symptoms of it. The true penitent will bring forth fruits meet for repentance. The man who is born of the Spirit, will know the things of the Spirit, and will lead a spiritual life. If he be renewed in the image of him that created him, he will evidence this by his knowledge, righteousness, and holiness. If he loves Christ, he will keep his commandments. If his heart is with God, his person will not usually be found in the company of the wicked. If he loves him that begat, he will also love them that are begotten, and prefer their company and conversation to that of all others. In short, if there be a real change of heart, it will manifest itself in the life. In some instances, arising from particular circumstances, there may be difficulty; and if, after much prayer and necessary investigation, a church is deceived in any instance, it is not guilty. I dare say if the members of a church would take as much trouble in this, as they do in giving out their money upon interest, they would seldom be deceived. They are not apt, out of excessive charity, to hazard it with a man of a merely specious appearance, till they enquire minutely into his circumstances and character.

OBJECTION 2.—I have heard some allege, "that if they would go to such strictness, they could admit very few."

I perfectly agree with them in this sentiment; but this objection is not an alleviation, but a dreadful aggravation of the crime. Such pastors are building a Babel, not a temple of God. When their work will be tried by the fire of the great day, it will be burned up, and they shall sustain a dreadful loss; and be saved, admitting they are the disciples of Christ, with the utmost difficulty. But this is not the remedy, but the very cause of their fewness. If a church is once formed upon the apostolical model, and walking in the commandments and ordinances of the Gospel, it is impossible but they will increase. Though at first they should be no more than a dozen, the Lord will be adding daily to them, such *as are saved.* The presence of Christ shall be with them, and continuing in prayer, they shall be multiplied; for whatever two of them agree in asking, they shall receive. I am convinced, from experience, that this is the case. Since I ceased to prostitute the Lord's supper at home and abroad, my labours have been more visibly blessed, and I have had more evidence of a work of grace going on, than I had in the whole five years of my ministry; and I am convinced that if a Gospel church is formed amongst us, and ruled by the laws of Christ, we shall have still more promising prospects. But be this as it may, as to myself, I hope I would not again administer the Lord's supper in the same promiscuous way, for any earthly consideration.

OBJECTION 3.—It is said, that "this sort of strictness will drive sinners away from the Gospel altogether, and therefore will defeat its own end."

What a pity that Christ had not the benefit of the advice of these sage counsellors! he would not have given a command so contrary to his own intention. Such objectors may have an orthodox creed, but the objection arises out of presumption and unbelief. Not to mention that the rejection of unregenerate persons, is often overruled to their conversion, our business is to obey God, and leave events to himself. Have we a greater interest, or are we more heartily concerned in enlarging his church, than he is himself? He hath the hearts of all men in his hands, and he turneth them as rivers of waters. He can make the most violent enemies, the most devoted friends of his Gospel, whenever he pleases. If he says, "Saul, Saul, why persecutest thou me?" the answer will be, "Lord, what wilt thou have me to do?" Every human invention to enlarge and support the Church of Christ, will not only utterly prove abortive, but generally will have a tendency directly the reverse of what is proposed. The great encouragement given to the heathen to renounce their religion, buried Christianity in a heap of rubbish, in the time of Constantine. And in every age the admission of impure members, to make a party respectable from their numbers, has had the worst effects. While the life of those that are spiritual is almost extinguished, the unregenerate become secure and hardened. Nothing can tend more effectually to retard the progress of the Gospel, and keep the eyes of the multitude continually blinded, than to give them the Christian name and privileges, whilst they are still the servants of Satan. They think they are safe, and believe they are Christians, though not so good as some others. If their minister is so faithful as to lay open their character in public, and show them their danger, they will either shuffle it off upon their neighbour, or apologise to themselves for their own conduct. Those who are accustomed to examine the hopes of sinners, will find that admission to what they call Christian privileges, is a very prevalent ground of hope. If all the churches of Christ were to treat the world as heathens, till they are born again, it would be a likely means in the hand of the Spirit to rouse them to inquiry, and lead them to repentance. Even those who are in the habit of refusing admission to persons of a scandalous character, very frequently do it in an improper manner. They ground their refusal, not upon their want of conversion, but their irregularities, or their not submitting to rules. This tends to mislead the sinner, and keep him ignorant of his real state; whereas, if he were faithfully told that his non-admission was the consequence of his want of the *new birth*, and not of the straitened rules of a party, he would be more likely to receive it with benefit, and even less irritation. Often the minister will throw the blame upon the session, and they again upon their rules, from a cowardly disposition, lest they should give offence. Thus the person is led to believe that the fault lies more in the straitness of their rules, than in himself. The placing of his admission or rejection upon his discharge of certain external duties, has the same mischievous effect. He is led to look on this, not as an evidence of his state, but as forming his title to heaven. One thing I would ask at those who make this objection, let them answer it candidly to their own conscience. Whether are you more afraid that this would lessen the Church of Christ, or *the stipend*? Whether are you more afraid of injuring the cause of Christ, or the credit of *your party*?

OBJECTION 4.—It is pleaded in defence of promiscuous communion, " that Judas was admitted to the Lord's table." Judas was once a pillar upon which I thought I could safely rest my defence; but since I have more maturely and impartially considered the matter, I have entirely given that up. We are never in a likely way to obtain truth as long as we are searching for a justification of our own conduct, rather than the mind of the Spirit. I am afraid that there are many who examine this question in this temper. A drowning man will catch at any twig before he will sink. Thus many, overwhelmed by positive Scripture precept, perhaps producing some qualms of conscience, catch at Judas to keep them above water. They do not see anything to extricate themselves from their difficulty, and because, in their present situation, they cannot comply, they too easily impose upon themselves, as to the sin of setting the Word of God at variance with itself. There is certainly a difficulty in determining whether Judas was, or was not, present at the institution of the supper. It would appear to me, from the most impartial examination of the Gospels which record the relation, that he was not. We know Scripture cannot contradict itself; and when it seems to do so, that analysis must be admitted, which is most conformable to the general tenor of the whole. If, then, there are innumerable passages to prove the duty of pure communion, and if the presence of Judas at the supper be contrary to this, that passage which seems to say he was, must be understood so as to agree with that which positively, or even apparently says he was not. I think also that Luke's account can more easily be explained in consistency with John's, than John's in consistency with the order of the narration of Luke. The inversion of order in the narration of facts, is no singular occurrence in the Gospels; but John states the fact positively, circumstantially, and minutely. John xiii. 30—"He then having received *the sop*,* went *immediately* out." To make Luke agree with this, we have nothing to do but what must be done in many other cases, to suppose an inversion of order in the narration. But this I mention, rather to reconcile the evangelists, than to support my argument in the point under debate. I do not think, that in order to prove the duty of pure communion, there is any necessity to exclude Judas from the first supper. What was Judas? He was a polished

---

* This was in eating the passover.

hypocrite. What is a hypocrite? Not a man who pretends to be religious, signs an orthodox creed, and leads a heterodox life, but a man to all human appearance a real Christian, and for a time walking as one, though in heart and in the sight of God an impenitent sinner. Such was Judas. There was not a more plausible character among the apostles than this very man. None of his brethren suspected him more than themselves. Even when our Lord declared that one of them should betray him, their language was not "Lord is it Judas?" but, "Lord, is it I?" Now, such characters might be in any church without the smallest blame being attachable to either church rulers, or church members. If the church receives them as real Christians, it is guiltless, though they are like Judas. This, however, is no apology for those who admit carnal men, who discover no evidence of conversion, nay frequently of whom they have no hopes at all. It is argued, that though Judas was a hypocrite, yet that our Lord knew him to be such. A fact most unquestionable; but our Lord's omniscience is no rule of conduct for us, nor did he act according to it in many other cases. He had various and important reasons for choosing this hypocrite to the apostleship, and the same might he have had for allowing him to take his seat at his supper. Our Lord, by acting as the administrator of this ordinance, had no need to avail himself of his omniscience, by forbidding Judas to partake; because in this he could have been no example to us, as we had not the same means of detecting hypocrites. Besides, he might design to show us, that if such characters as Judas would afterwards get admission into any of his churches, they would be blameless. The guilt, in this matter, is not in receiving hypocrites, but in retaining them, after they discover their true character. Judas, the hypocrite, might be a church member, but Judas the betrayer, never was, nor could be. Granting everything, then, that the abettors of impure communion themselves can demand from the case of Judas, to what does it amount? that a hypocrite may be admitted to the Lord's table without sin in the church. Will any say that because Christ knew this man to be an hypocrite, that therefore we may admit persons whom *we* know to be hypocrites; if we know them to be hypocrites, then they are no longer hypocrites; for we cannot know this as Christ knew it, by looking into their hearts, but from their discovering this by their lives and conversation. The case of Judas cannot fairly be drawn any farther. Besides, if it be alleged to justify the admission of members who give evidence that they are not partakers of the grace of the Gospel, it will set Christ the master, and Paul the servant at variance. The latter positively commands them not so much as eat with one who is called a brother, when once he discovers an inconsistency between his character and profession—1 Cor. v. 11. Timothy is strictly charged to withdraw from those " who had a *form* of godliness, but denied the power thereof."

But can there be anything more truly ridiculous than for those who justify impure communion by the example of Judas, to spend whole hours in debarring and fencing? If our Lord did not debar Judas, and if this shows the propriety of admitting persons whom we know to be unworthy, the conclusion is, that it would be improper to forbid them. If the sober *worldling* is admitted, I ask by what authority is the drunkard, the swearer, the fornicator, &c., denied admission? Ah! brethren, you must be at a great loss for a foundation, when you are obliged to build upon Judas. It must be an ill-built house, in which Judas himself is the chief cornerstone.

OBJECTION 5.—The parable of the tares and the wheat, is usually one of the bulwarks of impure churches.* But this objection is founded on a misapplication of the parable. It supposes that the field is the church, whereas our Lord himself expressly explains it to mean

* For a full, clear, and satisfactory explanation of this parable, see "Mr. Innes' Reasons for separating from the Church of Scotland." I decline a full explanation of this, and some other things, as they are largely treated in that pamphlet, which I think should be in the hands of all who wish for information on the subject.

the *world*. The tares are considered as church members; whereas, this would make our Lord's injunction contrary to that of the apostle Paul, " Purge out the old leaven." " Do ye not judge them that are within." It was also the devil who sowed them, and not Christ's servants by mistake. Those, who from this, plead for promiscuous admission, acknowledge themselves to be, not the servants of Christ, but of Satan, employed in sowing the tare-seed in Christ's field, while his servants sleep. But without spending time in showing why it cannot have this interpretation, I will just briefly point out what I take to be its obvious and consistent meaning. The wheat represents the children of God; the tares the children of the wicked one; they both grow in the same field, the *world*. The servants of Christ are not to endeavour to root out the latter, lest in doing so, they would root out the wheat. The design of the parable, is to show the impropriety of persecution, from this reason, that if the wicked of one generation were cut off, thousands of the children of God, who are to spring from them, would thereby be prevented from coming into being. The lives of the wicked are now preserved, because they are the ancestors of multitudes, who shall turn to God in the latter days. This I take to be also the meaning of Matt. xxiv. 22—" For the *elect's sake*, those days shall be shortened." By *elect* here, we are, in my opinion, principally to understand the *unborn* elect. The Jews, who escaped at the siege of Jerusalem, were spared, because they were to be the fathers of all those Jews who shall turn to God in the restoration. God could have preserved the elect that were alive in the time of that siege, in various ways. But what other way could the prophecies of the restoration of the Jews, have been accomplished, than by preserving a number of that wicked generation, for the purpose of introducing his future people into existence? If all the Jews had been cut off then, what would have become of those countless thousands and millions of their descendents, that shall serve Christ in their return? The Jews, since their rejection of Christ, have been preserved, perhaps *chiefly* for the sake of their future offspring. This is clearly expressed in the prophecy of Isaiah lxv. 8. As the unripe bunch of grapes is preserved for the sake of the wine that it shall afterwards yield, so God preserves the Jewish nation for the sake of their future descendents, who are to serve him.

CHAPTER XII.

ADDITIONAL REASONS FOR SEPARATING FROM THE GENERAL SYNOD.

THOUGH I had no objection to the government of classical Presbytery, and could effect purity of communion in my own congregation, without experiencing any hindrance from foreign interference, still I could not with a good conscience remain a member of the General Synod. I have many reasons for this conviction; a few of them I will here state.

1. "How can a man mount a very high hill with a weighty burthen, having several hundreds pulling him back by the skirts? Is it not much better to climb up the precipice in company with others who are going the same way, to go arm in arm, the strong bearing the weak, so that if a foot slip, we may not be dashed to pieces by a fall?" The former was exactly my situation; the whole weight of my connection being as a clog upon me, retarding my progress, by their laws, example, and spirit. We have all too much inclination to indifference and negligence in our Lord's cause. There is no need of any external hindrance. "Can a man take fire into his bosom, and not be burned?" Who will say, that the very society of men indifferent to religion, is not a strong temptation to relax exertion in the cause of Christ? But especially, if they are not only indifferent but inimical to the spreading of the Gospel, the danger is increased. If the religion of the Bible be called enthusiasm and madness, there is a strong temptation to hide its peculiar features, and appear less zealous for its diffusion. "Two cannot walk together except they are agreed." What concord, then, can there be between them and me? They view me with jealousy, and I consider them traitors to my

Master.* My exertions for a revival of religion they think useless. Some suppose that I am actuated by a love of applause, while others, more friendly, think I am only mad. Now, in this situation, what mutual happiness can there be from the society of men so opposite in their views and conduct? We both contribute to make each other uncomfortable. I am sure I have never suffered more acute pain in my life, than in their assemblies. I avoided their meetings as much as I could, for I always entered them with horror and reluctance. But of late, I understand they have determined that I should not enjoy that liberty. Is it not, then, much better that I should act separately, for I am sure they are not more offensive to me, than I am to them? Shall I, for a morsel of bread, sacrifice my own happiness, and remain under continual restraint and temptation? "A man's life consisteth not in the abundance of the things he possesses." He must be a very inexperienced Christian indeed, who thinks that he does not need rather to be spurred than curbed in his course.

2. "I cannot be a member of the General Synod, without renouncing my Christian liberty, and submitting my conscience to be ruled and lorded over by man." I am not allowed to be directed by my own conscience in the service of my Master. I must act not on my own conviction of what is right and wrong, but according to the caprice of others; nay of those I esteem as decided enemies to the cause of the Lord Jesus. I might get drunk frequently; associate with the most profligate; spend the sabbath afternoons in gay parties; follow the world the whole week with my whole heart; preach against the peculiar doctrines of revelation; deny the very Lord and Saviour of men; attend the theatre, balls, and card parties; and still my

---

* When I involve the Synod in a general censure, I always intend a majority of the members, and not every individual, because a majority is the Synod, and can rule the minority as they please. I pretend not to determine what may be the number of faithful servants of Christ in that connection. For such, whatever be our difference of opinion, I have the most cordial affection.

brethren would extend their charity to me; except a formal charge would be brought against me by my own congregation, I might even pass unnoticed. Here human frailty, and freedom of inquiry would plead my excuse. But if I would dare to preach the Gospel out of my own bounds, or admit an evangelical minister of another denomination to occupy my pulpit, dreadful would be the thunder that would be hurled against me! Nothing less than public rebuke for the first, and suspension for the second commission of such *mortal sins*. "Whereas it appears, that our laws respecting the admission of men, not members of this body, or licentiates under its care, to officiate for us, are too generally expressed to be of any practical use: It is now enacted, that no man, not a member of this body, or a licentiate under its care (the Presbytery of Antrim, and southern association excepted), shall be permitted to officiate for us in our congregations, until he shall first submit his credentials to the Presbytery, in whose bounds he wishes to preach, and until he shall be approved of by the Presbytery; and any minister of this body, violating this law, shall, for the first offence, be publicly rebuked by his Presbytery, before his congregation, and for the second be suspended *ab officio, sine die*." If ever a child was known by its resemblance to the parent, this sure must be the daughter of the mother of harlots. This is her prominent feature; this is her very temper and genius. "O, ye Scribes and Pharisees, how long will ye make void the law of God by your traditions! In vain do you worship him, teaching for doctrines the commandments of men." Where is their authority for imposing such restraints upon the servants of the Lord? I cannot submit to this tyranny without calling men my master, contrary to the express command of Jesus. I am commanded "to stand fast in the liberty with which Christ has made me free." Though the apostle speaks this immediately of the Jewish yoke, yet, as no Scripture is of any private interpretation, it equally forbids any human imposition, in the things of God. When Christ has left us free, we are not to allow any man or body of men to bind us, or even to bind ourselves. Every human restraint in religion is usurpation and treason. A Christian, indeed, is sometimes to decline using his liberty, to avoid stumbling his weak brother, but he is not even in this case to come under bondage to him, still less is he to come under restraint to please those who are enemies to the *pure Gospel of salvation.*

I am truly concerned for the spiritual darkness of my native land. While the work of the Lord is flourishing in both parts of Britain, there is in this island as yet but little done. Ah! the thousands that are perishing for lack of knowledge! What profligacy of manners do we see everywhere abounding! I am convinced that there is no other remedy for the evil but the *unadulterated Gospel of Christ.* Shall I then submit to be cooped up in a corner, and restrained by human fetters from lending a hand to rescue my brethren from the pit of destruction? "Time is short;" the day of work is but a blink; I must soon give an account of my stewardship, and I know that however much I may incur the displeasure of men, however great may be my temporal loss, in the end I shall not repent the step I have taken. I know that God judgeth not as man judgeth. I know, indeed, it is said that I might employ all my time in my own congregation; but I answer, that I may do much abroad, and not do the less at home. I believe we will generally find, that those who do most abroad, likewise do most in their own congregation. It is my duty to feed the poor of my own neighbourhood rather than those at a distance; but it would be a hard matter, if I was so bound that I could not give a halfpenny to a starving beggar on my journey. Besides, the public preaching of the Gospel is that part of the office in which I take peculiar delight, and in which I am never weary. The hireling may work his hours, but he that loves Jesus, should, like him, " go about doing good;" like him it should be his very "meat and drink, to do the will of his heavenly Father."

3. "I do not find myself justified in recognizing as ministers, those whom I consider as destitute of the qualifications deemed essential by an apostle." A bishop must be blameless, the husband of one wife,

vigilant, sober, of good behaviour, given to hospitality, apt *(rather fit) to teach—not given to wine—no striker—* not *greedy of filthy lucre,* but patient—not a brawler, nor *covetous—*one that ruleth well his own house, having his children in subjection with all gravity. (For if a man know not how to rule his own house, how shall he take care of the church of God?) Not a *novice,* lest being lifted up with pride, he fall into the condemnation of the devil. Moreover, he must have *a good report of them which are without,* lest he fall into reproach and the snare of the devil"—1 Tim. iii. 2-7. " A bishop must not be self willed—*not soon angry—a lover of good men—just, holy, temperate—holding fast the faithful Word,* as he hath been taught, that he may be able, by sound doctrine, both to exhort and convince the gainsayers"—Titus i. 7-9. I forbear to make the application. Suffice it to say, that if these are essential qualifications in a pastor, I cannot recognise as brethren many of the members of the General Synod.

4. " A Calvanist and a Socinian or Arian, can with no propriety worship together." They do not address the same God. When they unite in prayer, they are like a friend to the Pretender, and another of King George, drinking *the king,* as a toast, when each intended his own favourite. They do not address the same being, though they use the same name. If I address the Father, Son, and Holy Ghost, as my God, he that denies the Godhead of the Son and Spirit, must look upon me as an idolater. In return, I look upon him as an atheist. " He that denieth the Son, the same hath not the Father; he that honoureth not the Son, honoureth not the Father that hath sent him." When he prayeth, he addresses not the Jehovah of the Scripture, but an idol of his own creation, as different from the true God, as Jupiter or Apollo.* His god

---

* The same thing will hold against making any unregenerate man the organ of prayer. When such men are set up to offer the prayers of an assembly, as they "know not God," so " they worship they know not what." They cannot pray with the Spirit, and consequently they cannot pray at all. Those who join them are partakers in their abominations.

is as really of his own making, as if he had hewn him out of wood or stone. He steals from the Scripture account of the true God, some of his properties, and those attributes that suit him best. When he robs him of his justice, and abusively extends his mercy, he can dispense with the sacrifice of Jesus; he has got a god to his mind; an idol of his own imagination. This god he loves, because this god does not hate sin; but the Jehovah of the Scriptures he hates, because he is the enemy of sin, and "hath revealed his wrath against all ungodliness and unrighteousness of men." In what then are we agreed? Not even in the God we worship: not in the way of salvation. How improper is it, then, for us to make each other the organ of prayer! How can we co-operate, seeing our principles are so entirely opposite? If each of us be conscientious, we must be at constant war. With as great propriety, might the French and English officers meet in a council of war, before an engagement, to concert the measures that each were to adopt, as people of such opposite sentiments to sit in the same Synod.

5. "By remaining in connection with the Synod, I contribute to deceive the public, as to the radical difference between my principles, and those maintained by many in the Synod." My example by continuing in that connection, might be the means of keeping some of the people of Christ under the ministry of those who corrupt the Gospel. It is natural for people to judge that there cannot be any momentous points in which we differ, or we would not continue to co-operate and acknowledge each other as brethren in Christ. This I know to be the case. The generality of private Christians in the General Synod, have no conception that we differ so materially. Suppose, then, I could remain a member of Synod, without injury to myself, yet I am guilty of deceiving others. If I think that any ministers of that body are wolves in sheep's clothing, not feeding, but devouring the flock, I am a partaker of their soul-murder, if I do not give the alarm, and warn the sheep to fly.

What is the use of the 8th chap. of 1 Cor. to us? Does it not teach us, that if in any particular instance, the use of our Christian liberty may prove an occasion of stumbling to weak brethren, we ought to forego it, rather than that they should be injured? If I sit in the idol's temple, eating the flesh of animals offered in sacrifice, though I eat it simply to satisfy my hunger, knowing that there is no divinity in the idol, and that the meat cannot be rendered in itself impure, by this improper use, yet my weak brother seeing me there, partaking with idolators, is led to think, that I am joining them in their worship, and by my example, is emboldened to eat it as a sacrifice to the idol.— "Through my knowledge, shall the weak brother perish, for whom Christ died?" Suppose, then, that my connection with the Synod was a matter not sinful in itself, yet by its consequences, it becomes sinful. Many may be encouraged by my example, to sit under a ministry, in which the Gospel is depraved, or hidden. If I should be the occasion of stumbling one of Christ's little ones, the loss I would sustain in the day of the Lord Jesus, would be infinitely greater than all I can lose by leaving the Synod. Awful will be our responsibility, and it is required, above all things, in a steward, that he be faithful. If this be not a lawful application of Scripture, I know of no use that this chapter can be at present.

6. "My connection with the Synod, is contrary to the law of love, and the duty I owe the members of it as men." If I believe, that "Except a man be born again, he cannot see the kingdom of God;" and if I believe that few of them evidence such a change; nay, if I know many of them to deny and ridicule this truth as enthusiasm, I would not be their friend, if in anything my conduct would lead them to believe, that I considered their situation to be less dangerous, than in reality I know it to be. Now, as long as I remain a member of Synod, and act with them as brethren in Christ, it is impossible for them to think that I am really in earnest, as to the importance of my views of the truths of the Gospel. Besides, there are many who would subscribe perhaps every doctrine of the Gospel, of whose state I have no better hopes. Such persons,

then, would have reason to complain of me in the judgment of the great day, that I acted an unfriendly part towards them; that while I considered them as " in the gall of bitterness and bond of iniquity," I acted with them as ministers of Christ; by which means they were led to conclude that I could have no very unfavourable opinion of them. I know I will be charged with a want of *charity of sentiment* when I express such an opinion of the Synod. Charity, however, is not a matter of opinion, but of feeling, and a man may have the purest love for another, while he is most strongly convinced of his guilt and danger. A juror may have every wish that the criminal may be acquitted, yet he may, by evidence, be obliged to join in the verdict "*guilty.*" Shall I go past my neighbour's house at night, seeing it on fire, and not awake him, lest I should disturb or grieve him? Shall I rather suffer him to be consumed in the flames, than alarm him? Yet this is the murderous charity for which many plead; that, while we have the clearest evidence that men are living without God, we should believe, or feign to believe, that they may be saved in their sins. In other words, we hope God is a liar—that he will not do as he has said. Dr. Johnson said that every man was to be held unlearned, till he proved the contrary. The observation is equally just when applied to religion. No man has a right to be esteemed a Christian, till his fruits prove it. What would we think of the man who would say, that in the judgment of charity, he looked upon all, or the greater part of men to be learned? The same should we think of the man who professes to believe, that men are Christians, who give no evidence of the fact. We have the word of unerring wisdom, declaring that all men are "by nature the children of wrath;" until we have evidence that they are born again, and adopted into the family of God, we are not warranted to look upon them as Christians. Eternal life is the worst I wish to any member of the Synod, or to any man on earth; but if I believe God, I must believe that all " who *know not God*, and *obey not the Gospel* of our Lord Jesus Christ, shall be punished with everlasting destruction from the presence of the Lord, and from the glory of his power.

7. "I cannot conscientiously join in licensing and ordaining those whom I know do not possess the prerequisite qualifications, pointed out in the Word of God." Paul states these minutely to Timothy and Titus. I do not think that it is right to give our countenance to any candidates, who do not answer to this description. The candidate for " the office of a bishop," must not be even a *novice*, or *new convert*, lest from his inexperience he should fall into temptation from the natural pride of the human heart.* But if it be improper to appoint *newly converted men* to the charge of a flock, how dreadful must be the sin of appointing the blind to lead the blind, and unregenerate men to feed the flock of Christ? Paul says to Timothy (1. Tim. v. 22), "Lay hands suddenly upon no man, neither be partaker of other men's sins: keep thyself pure." It appears, then, that those who give their sanction to unworthy men to preach the Gospel, are partakers of their sins. They share with them in the guilt of all the evil they commit in destroying the souls of men. He does not direct him to ordain no man without subscribing a human confession of faith. This could have been done in an instant; if this had been the test, there would have been no need of delay. The caution implies not only that Timothy should not ordain persons of a scandalous character, but even that persons who seemed to possess the requisite qualifications, should not be appointed to the pastoral office, till they had given sufficient evidences that they were what they seemed to be. All unregenerate men are the servants of Satan; and let them *subscribe* and *swear* what they will, Satan they will serve, " until they are turned from darkness unto light, and from the power of Satan unto God." How dreadful, then, is the crime of giving a

* Those who justify the appointment of unconverted men to preach the Gospel, and take charge of a church of Christ, from the example of Judas, would do well to consider the import of this portion of Scripture. If a man newly converted be unfit for the pastor's office, much more is he who is not converted at all.

public sanction to such men, as the servants of Christ! They will preach orthodoxy or heterodoxy as best suits their temporal interest, but though they have *the form* they have none of the power of godliness. They may preach a dead, dry system, but being blind, they cannot lead the blind; and having no spiritual organs to "discern the things of the Spirit, they cannot know them." I acknowledge the most conscientious may be deceived, but it is really awful to hear some good men pleading for the propriety of sending out unconverted men to preach the Gospel, because Judas was a hypocrite. It is no wonder, then, that some sects, with all their boasted orthodoxy, have little more of the life and power of godliness than those who do not make such high pretensions. Once acknowledge the principle that the servants of Satan, if they are orthodox and sober, are proper persons to feed the flock of Christ, and in a short time deadness and torpor will pervade the body. All the zeal of individuals will not be able to keep it alive. A profession of orthodoxy was not the test used by the apostles. "And when James, and Cephas, and John, who seemed to be pillars, *perceived the grace that was given unto me*, they gave to me and Barnabas the right hand of fellowship, that we should go unto the heathen, and they unto the circumcision"— Gal. ii. 9. The evidence of his qualifications was not the *subscription of a formula*, but *his appearing to have received the grace of God*. I cannot see how an unconverted orthodox minister is a less dangerous man than he who is most openly hostile to the doctrines of the Gospel. In my opinion, the former is the more dangerous of the two, as men are less aware of him. Paul, speaking of the deacons (1 Tim. iii. 10), says, "Let these also first be proved." This shows the great care that should be taken in choosing church officers. Their acknowledgment of the leading doctrines of the Gospel is not given as a test. Even persons that appear to possess the necessary qualifications, are not to be hastily appointed to office; *they must be proved.* "These also," that is, deacons as well as pastors. If this reasoning be just, it is applicable to all the denominations of Presbyterians, with which I am acquainted. But I am not obliged to rest any part of this argument upon the sinfulness of licensing and ordaining merely *unconverted men*. As a member of the General Synod, I may be forced to join in licensing and ordaining men whose *characters* and *doctrines* I condemn. I may be obliged to be the very organ of licensing and ordaining a man who preaches an opposite Gospel from what I believe to be true. What a monstrous inconsistency is here! If I believe the doctrines I preach, I must be convinced that I am sending out a murderer instead of a physician. Am I not guilty, then, of all the blood he spills? Surely I am partaker of this man's sins. Yes, I take shame and confusion of face to myself, that I have so long sanctioned my Master's enemies. I acknowledge myself to have hitherto been a partaker of the guilt of those who are the "enemies of the cross of Christ, whose God is their belly, whose glory is their shame, who mind earthly things."

8. "I have a positive and express command to separate from a corrupt church." 2 Cor. vi. 14–18— "Be ye not unequally yoked together with unbelievers, for what fellowship hath righteousness with unrighteousness? And what communion hath light with darkness? And what concord hath Christ with Belial? or what part hath he that believeth with an infidel? And what agreement hath the temple of God with idols? for ye are the temple of the living God; as God hath said, I will dwell in them and walk in *them ;* and I will be their God and they shall be my people. Wherefore come out from among them, and be ye separate, saith the Lord, and touch not the unclean *thing*, and I will receive you. And will be a Father unto you, and ye shall be my sons and daughters, saith the Lord Almighty." The Corinthians are here commanded to separate from their unbelieving and idolatrous neighbours; to abandon their worship, and form no intimate alliances of any kind with them. This command is given to me as well as to the Corinthians, for I am no otherwise addressed but as a member of the apostolical churches. All unconverted men are idolators, and unbelievers, and a connection with them

is even more dangerous in a country called Christian, than in a heathen country. The same reason also that forbids the marriage of believers with unbelievers, will equally forbid our connection in church communion with such. It is also exceedingly obvious, that though the command is particularly levelled against joining in the idolatrous worship of the heathens, it is expressed in a general manner, so as to include the view I now give of it, as literally, and with as strict precision, as the other. " Be ye not unequally yoked together with unbelievers." This will hold not only in this or that instance, but is universally applicable to the formation of any intimate union of believers with unbelievers, especially in church communion. Besides, there is not an argument here used to show the impropriety of this union, but what equally applies in this view. All believers are righteous, all unbelievers are unrighteous. All believers are light, all unbelievers are darkness. Christ dwells in all believers; Belial dwells in all unbelievers; he is the spirit that now worketh in the children of disobedience. Unbelievers of every description have different views, objects of pursuit, pleasures, and aversions, from believers. They have no common ground upon which they can found an intimate union. Every believer is a temple of God, which he inhabits through the spirit; idols of one kind or other inhabit the heart of every unbeliever. I would just further observe, that if some of those who have long successfully quoted this portion of Scripture to show the duty of separating from the General Synod, would look a little more narrowly into it, they might find that they should carry their separation to a greater length. I think it fairly condemns the admission of all carnal men to church communion. It is a union of believers with unbelievers, not merely of orthodox with heterodox, which is here forbidden. " Be ye not unequally yoked together with unbelievers."

A similar command have I in Rev. xviii. 4.—" Come out of her my people, that ye be not partakers of her sins, and that ye receive not of her plagues." This indeed is immediately spoken of the mother of harlots, but it will equally hold with respect to each of her daughters. If we are to leave one corrupt church, we are certainly to leave another. If our remaining in communion with the spiritual Babylon would make us partakers of her sins, and subject us to share her plagues, the same reasoning will prove that we are partakers of the sins of any corrupt church with which we are connected. If we must come out of the one to free us from her sins, the same thing will be necessary with respect to every other. As long as we countenance them we are sharers of their guilt, and liable to share their punishment.

Paul gives Timothy (2 Tim. iii. 1–5) a list of characters who would assume a profession of religion, without the power of it. From these, he positively commands him to "turn away." Now, if there be any such characters evidently in the General Synod, it is equally my duty to withdraw from them. This is another passage which the advocates of impure ministerial and Christian communion would do well to consider. These might be very orthodox men; they had a "form of godliness." They would have no objection to subscribe the Westminster Confession. Most of them appear also, not to have been openly immoral. They might have a very sanctified air in a church court. Yet from such, there is a peculiar necessity to withdraw; from such there is a peculiar danger. When men of such a character appear, and are acknowledged in a church of Christ, "the times are perilous." The devout worldling is more dangerous than the openly profane. Timothy is also commanded to withdraw from every teacher who would teach otherwise than the apostle had directed, "and consent not to wholesome words, even the words of our Lord Jesus Christ, and to the doctrine which is according to godliness," 1 Tim. vi. 3–5. Certainly, then, I am not justifiable in remaining in connection with the General Synod.

In writing to the Church of the Thessalonians, Paul gives them this charge: "Now I command you, brethren, in the name of our Lord Jesus Christ, that ye withdraw yourselves from every brother that walketh disorderly, and not after the tradition which he received of us." What Christ speaks to a church in general, is spoken to each individual, in particular. Though classical Presbytery were of God's appointing, yet, if there were but one disorderly member in the General Synod, and I could not get him removed, it would be my duty to withdraw; otherwise I am a partaker of his sins. As long as I am a member of that body, I am an accomplice with every irregular person in it, whether minister or private member.* We are positively commanded to "have no fellowship with the unfruitful works of darkness, but to reprove them"—Eph. v. 11. This precept we can never obey, while we hold professed communion with unbelievers. Nay, so far from holding communion with them in the ordinances of Christ, we are not even allowed to have a friendly intimacy with those that are called brethren, if their characters belie their profession. This would be a scandal to the religion of Christ, and would give occasion to the wicked to blaspheme. I cannot, then, be a member of the General Synod and an obedient servant of Christ.

* If there be any justice in this remark, it is a considerable argument against an associated church government. We would, in that case, be accountable for the conduct of those of whom we could not possibly have any knowledge.

CHAPTER XIII.

OBJECTIONS ANSWERED.

HAVING in the last chapter given some reasons for separating from a corrupt church, I will conclude this pamphlet by taking notice of a few objections that have been frequently urged upon me, to dissuade me from giving up my connection with the General Synod.

1. "It is said that a material error prevailed in the churches of Galatia, and that in writing to them, the apostle does not command one part of them to separate from the other, upon the supposition that the majority would not return to the truth—that in case the majority of the Corinthian church had taken part with the incestuous man, and refused to obey the apostolical injunction, Paul gives no command to the minority to separate from the majority—and that our Lord, in reproving the churches of Asia, does not command any separation of individuals, in case the greater part in any church might not return to their duty."

With respect to each of these instances, I answer, that there is not one of them parallel to my situation. These churches, with all their declensions and corruptions, were still churches of Christ, apostolically constituted, and the bulk of them real, though censurable saints. Consequently, when their errors would be laid before them, they would unite in correcting them. But the matter is widely different with respect to a church neither upon the apostolical model, nor constituted of members like those of the apostolical churches. As to the churches of Galatia, there was no room to give any such command. The apostle says (Gal. v. 10), "I have confidence in you, through the Lord Jesus, that you will be none otherwise minded." If he had such an opinion of them, and believed that they would comply with his injunctions, where would have been the propriety of giving a command of separation to the few, in case of the disobedience of the many? The error of the judaizing teachers, had indeed infected the body, so that the apostle found it necessary to express his doubt of them;* but he had confidence that they would return to the truth when he called them to it. Nay, he supposeth the whole matter to arise from a very few; " but he that troubleth you, shall bear his judgment, whosoever he be." "I would they were even cut off that trouble you." "A little leaven leaveneth the whole lump." Here he counts upon the allegiance of the great bulk of the members of the churches, and even intimates his wish, that the authors of this false doctrine should be cut off. In what, then, does this countenance the remaining in a corrupt church? Nay, it is directly against it. The apostle knew that the greatest part of them would return to the truth, therefore could not suppose it necessary to advise individuals to separate, upon the supposition that it would be otherwise. But the few that spread this doctrine, he advises to be cut off. This shows us what we should do with those who trouble a church with false doctrines. They are not, out of false lenity, to be suffered to remain and corrupt the body, but removed as morbid members.

This objection is entirely founded upon an improper conception of the nature of a church of Christ, judging of it as a wordly society, in which the majority is supposed to be the whole, and is enabled to direct all its proceedings. But it is not numbers, but the *obedient*, that constitute the church, whether they be the majority or minority. Had all the members in any one of the Galatian churches, except two or three, resolved to retain their error, in contempt of the apostolic authority, to these two or three obedient disciples, the apostle's direction was still given, "I would that they were cut off that trouble you." Obedience is the test of discipleship. Had the majority of any of these churches, refused to obey, the obedient few were bound to "cut off" the

---

* Even this doubting shows what he formerly took them to be, when organized as a church.

disobedient many. Those few, go where they would, were still the church.

Indeed if it be a duty to " cut off " one or a few disorderly and troublesome members, it will still be more so with respect to many. There is not one argument why three thousand should cut off three which will not prove that three should cut off three thousand, with an accession of strength proportioned to the increase of numbers. " If a little leaven leaveneth the whole lump," if not purged out there still is greater reason to dread, that the leavened mass will soon infect a few particles. If a whole church is in danger from one, two, or three; one, two, or three, must be in much greater danger from a corrupt body. What is the reason of cutting off one disorderly member? Is it not lest he bring a scandal upon the religion of Christ; be a stumbling block to weak Christians; infect the body; become an offence to unbelievers; and to reclaim the individual. Each of these reasons will derive additional strength when applied to numbers.

The same reasoning will hold good with respect to the Church of Corinth, and the churches of Asia. The apostle addressed the Corinthians as " saints sanctified in Christ Jesus;" and everywhere through his epistle considers them as true believers, though in many respects greatly to blame. How, then, could he suppose that they would not obey him? This would have been as if the king would send an order to the House of Commons to try one of their members for some improper language or conduct, at the same time applauding the members for their fidelity and zeal, and then add, " yet if a majority unite to screen the offender, let the faithful minority protest." How incongruous would such language be? Yet not more so than what such objectors would expect from the apostle. After all, I will suppose that the whole Church of Corinth had taken part with the incestuous person against the apostle, except one, two, or three, still it would have been the duty of such to have withdrawn from the disorderly society, which no more deserved the name of a church of Christ, than a congregation of Mussulmen. The few that obeyed the apostle were the church, and to them the command was given. 1 Cor. v. 4—"In the name of our Lord Jesus Christ, when ye are gathered together, and my Spirit, with the power of our Lord Jesus Christ, to deliver such an one," &c. The offender, and all who sided with him, were to be removed as disorderly brethren. The same may be said as to the case of the Asiatic churches. To the very worst of them Christ said, "As many as I love, I rebuke and chasten." They were much to blame, but with all their faults they were true churches of Christ. Nay, the very accusations Christ alleged against them, not only show the bulk of them to be saints, but prove the necessity of pure communion, and of cutting off impure members. He blames some of them for having the propagators of false doctrines among them. This shows that a church is to purge out the old leaven, and become a new lump. And if he blames them for having a few false teachers among them, how much more has he had occasion to blame me, for continuing so long with a corrupt body? With what propriety, then, can a Christian allege the state of these churches to justify his continuance in corrupt societies? With what face can any church allege this, to justify impure communion? If these apostolical churches had any improper member among them, they are not praised; they are not held excusable; they are severely reprimanded for it.

2. Another objection is, " that I give up an important station. I cowardly desert the field of battle, and in all probability deprive myself for ever of an opportunity of preaching the Gospel. Now Paul says, 'woe unto me, if I preach not the Gospel.' Christ says, 'the harvest is plenteous and the labourers few.' It must then be highly improper to leave a ripe harvest without labourers to reap it."

What is the amount of this objection? It is "do evil that good may come." If I have shown that such a connection is sinful, no supposed advantages resulting to religion from it should have the smallest weight, because they are nothing in reality. What good could I do in any situation on earth, without God's blessing upon my labours? And is it supposable that I am likely to have this blessing, when I refuse to obey him? Before my attention was turned to this subject, when my views were not so clear, God might have partially blessed my labours. But I could no longer look for a blessing, nor with a good conscience preach the Gospel at all, while conscious that I was not complying with his will. "I leave an important situation." What sort of language in the mouth of a Christian? If I had an opportunity of preaching the Gospel in every parish in the Island, could I of myself call one sinner to repentance? A station is only important as there may be the probability of doing good, and I can see no probability of this, as long as we live in the willful neglect, or the breach of the least part of the known will of God. Ah! friends, I am afraid if we search our hearts to the bottom, the real motive of remaining in corrupt churches, is rather the importance of it to our own temporal interest, than a concern lest the work of the Lord should stand undone. "Sirs, ye know that by this craft we have our gain." But "I am running as a coward, out of the field of battle." No, I am only repairing to the standard of my Captain, and deserting his enemies. I am only putting myself in a situation in which I can fight without restraint, and whether I am to be an officer or a private, must be left to my General, who employs every man in the situation that suits him best, and in which he can render the most effectual service. But "is it not a sin for me to put myself out of a condition to preach the Gospel?" Yes, if I would give up preaching the Gospel for the most splendid throne in Europe, I would be unworthy of opening my mouth to proclaim the glad tidings of salvation. If I would quit my station for the sake of a little more of the *unrighteous mammon*, I would be inexcusable. If I would quit preaching for fear of man, "woe would be upon me." But if I quit a station by the command of my General, I am not to blame.

But "the harvest is great and the labourers are few." True, very true; and what is the consequence? Is it that I must transgress the orders of Christ to reap the harvest? Is there no way of obeying one command, without breaking another? Put the objection into words, and it will run thus: "O Lord, thou hast a great harvest and few to reap it; I am an active young labourer, but I cannot serve thee unless thou allowest me to break one of thy commandments. It is but a little one; and it is much better for thee to give me this liberty, than to want my services, for thou canst not do well without me. Thou must either take me on these terms, or thou must lose thy grain?" Were I to reason and act thus, the Lord of the harvest could soon lay me aside, and let me see, he could have the work done without me. It is for us to do what is duty, and leave events to God. If he has any work to do, at present in Ireland, I am sure I am taking the way to do it. If he has work to do, who is he most likely to employ as his instruments? Will he let me stand idle in the market-place, and employ others to serve him, whose sole object is to serve themselves? If it be my supreme delight to win souls to Christ, I do not think I shall be disappointed. If it be in any measure my meat and drink to do his will, it is not likely he will refuse to give me employment. "And whatever we ask we receive of him, because we keep his commandments, and do these things that are pleasing in his sight." "He that loveth me, keepeth my commandments." "Follow me, and I will make you fishers of men." "Ye are my friends, if ye do whatsoever I command you." "And why call ye me Lord, Lord, and do not the things which I say."

3. No argument hath been more frequently used to reconcile me to the Synod, than "the duty I owe my family. 'He that provideth not for his own, especially for those of his own household, hath denied the faith, and is worse than an infidel.'" I acknowledge the obligation of this Scripture in its fullest extent. But am I obliged to neglect one duty by attending to another? I am to provide for my family; but will any say, I should rob and murder to support them? I am to provide, but it is things that are lawful. I am not to support them at the expense of a good conscience. If I cannot trust my family upon God, how will I trust him with my soul? He hath not only said, "He that provideth not," &c., but he hath also said, "Seek ye first the kingdom of God and his righteousness, and all these

things shall be added unto you." I must either renounce the 6th chap. of Matthew, or I must do duty, and trust myself and family to him who feedeth the fowls of the air, and clothes the lilies of the field. He that feedeth his enemies will not suffer his friends to starve. With what conscience could I press others to trust in Providence, when I distrusted him myself? When I read the history of Aristides, the Athenian, and many other pagan sages, who scorned riches for earthly fame, I am ashamed that the glories of heaven, and the love of Jesus should have a slighter impression upon me. Cyrus was fed upon brown bread and cresses, to fit him for a consummate general; and shall I think it a grievance to submit to that discipline, to enable me more successfully to fight the battles of my Lord. I must "endure hardness, as a good soldier of Jesus Christ." Perhaps there never was a general of distinction, who has not undergone more hardships, fatigues, wants, and dangers, to procure temporal glory, than I have any prospect of in my more honourable warfare. "Now they do it for a corruptible crown, but we for an incorruptible." A few years hence, and all my wants and sorrows shall be no more. I will be where "the wicked cease from troubling, and the weary are at rest." "They that are wise shall shine as the brightness of the firmament, and they that turn many unto righteousness as the stars for ever and ever."

> And must I part with all I have,
>   My dearest Lord for thee?
> It is but right, since thou hast done
>   Much more than this for me.
>
> Yes, let it go—one look from thee,
>   Will more than make amends
> For all the losses I sustain,
>   Of credit, riches, friends.
>
> Ten thousand worlds, ten thousand lives,
>   How worthless they appear,
> Compar'd with thee supremely good,
>   Divinely bright and fair!
>
> Saviour of souls! could I from thee
>   A single smile obtain,
> Though destitute of all things else,
>   I'd glory in my gain.

A BIOGRAPHICAL SKETCH OF ALEXANDER CARSON (1776-1844)

BY

JOHN FRANKLIN JONES

A Biographical Sketch of Alexander Carson (1776-1844)

Alexander Carson—Irish Presbyterian-turned-Baptist, pastor, expositor, author—was born at Artrae, ("BS" 24) not far from Cookstown, Tyrone Country, Ireland in 1776 of a family of Scotch origin, who probably came to North Ireland during the reign of James 1. Converted at an early age, he graduated with first honors at Glasgow University and received the LL.D. from Bacon College, Kentucky (Cathcart).

He settled as a government-paid Presbyterian pastor at Tubbermore in 1798, (Armitage, 571). Tubbermore was a town of 500 surrounded by a large population of Scotch-Irish farmers (Cathcart).

Early in his ministry, he came to three Baptist principles which set him in opposition to the Presbyterians: that congregationalism was the Scriptural form of church government; that immersion was the New Testament mode of baptism; and that only believers should be baptized (Cathcart). Concerning the presbytery, he said: "Scripture presbytery is the eldership, or plurality of elders in a particular congregation" (*Answer to Ewing*, 382; Chapter 10, n. 8; cited by Armitage, 130).

Thereafter, he gave up his living, (Armitage, 571) and departed his congregation upon the testimony of his favorite hymn:

> And must I part with all I have,
> My dearest Lord, for thee?
> It is but right, since thou has done
> Much more than that for me.
>
> Yes, let it go, one look from thee
> Will more than make amends
> For all the losses I sustain
> Of Wealth, of credit, friends (Cathcart).

The Baptist church he started grew to 500 members in his lifetime. His reputation spread and among his lasting friends were the Haldanes—Robert and James—of Edinburgh (Cathcart).

Carson was a Greek scholar, a clear reasoner, a logician, and a philosopher, and possessed a piercing intelligence. His Presbyterian friends called him the "Jonathan Edwards of the nineteenth century" (Cathcart).

He was an expository preacher. Cathcart said: "Few ever heard him take a little text and suspend some weighty subject upon it by a slender connecting link" (Cathcart).

His earlier writings included a work on figures of speech, developing the self-evident principles on figures of speech which was regarded as a standard on the subject matter ("BS", 25).

Carson's intensive pastoral desire to promote holy living among his worldly and wayward parishioners. His initial warnings to his congregants about their dangers developed into a failed attempt at church discipline, then an appeal to the ecclesiastical courts of the Synod. He came to the conclusion that his only appeal lay in that spiritual appeal to the teachings and simple order of Scripture. Thereupon, he left the Synod of Ulster ("BS," 26-28).

His *Reasons for Leaving the Synod of Ulster* maintained via strong reasoning the independence of the primitive churches of the New Testament. That volume declared his insistence that his participation in the Synod was a surrender of his conscience to one other than Christ. He systematically argued that the form of church government most likely to be divine was (1) the one capable of the least abuse–independence; (2) the one most able to preserve purity of doctrine without human expedients; and (3) the one which most leads to, and compels church members to, Scripture itself ("BS," 28-29).

From his firm commitment to the Bible as the only law-book, he first adopted congregational order, then regenerate church membership, and finally, believer's baptism ("BS," 31,33). His *Baptism: Its Mode and Subject* was first published in London and later republished by the Baptist Publication Society, Philadelphia. Cathcart said of this work:

> His octavio volume on baptism is a masterpiece of learning and logic; it overthrows quibbles about the Abrahamic covenant, giving authority to baptize children, as old as Augustine of Hippo, and as wide-spread as Pedobaptist Christendom, and allegations that baptism might mean sprinkling or pouring, with as much ease as a horse, unaccustomed to a rider, hurls to the ground the little boy who has ventured to mount him (Cathcart, 187).

Regarding his dogmatic writing style, Cathcart continued:

> Truth coming forth like a defiant giant is more attractive than when it appears making simpering apologies for venturing to show its face, and to disturb the equanimity of error and wrong, though sturdy truth, carrying a sharp and needful sword in a sheath of love, pleases us most (Cathcart, 188).

While returning from delivering addresses to the Baptist Missionary Society, he fell into the dock at Liverpool in 1844. Though rescued, and continuing upon his journey to Belfast, he became ill during the night and died the next day after landing, August 24, 1844. Carson spent nearly fifty years in ministry

(Cathcart). Armitage called him "most illustrious of the Irish Baptists."

At his untimely death, Carson had completed all the necessary work for a treatise on the atonement. Among his stated, but unfulfilled, intentions was a book on the best mode of teaching the churches and the characteristic style of Scripture. He also left unpublished commentaries to the Galatians, Hebrews, and several smaller articles ("BS", 44-45).

His wife--the mother of his thirteen children–and some of his children, preceded him in death. One son died of brain fever simultaneously with his ordination to the pastoral office ("BS", 47-47)

BIBLIOGRAPHY

Armitage, Thomas. *A History of the Baptists; Traced by their Vital Principles and Practices, from the Time of Our Lord and Saviour Jesus Christ to the Year 1886.* With an introduction by J. L. M. Curry. New York: Bryan, Taylor, & Co. 1887.

"Biographical Sketch of Alexander Carson," in *Baptism in its Mode and Subjects*, by Alexander Carson, 13-47. London: Houlston & Stoneman, 1844.

Cathcart, William, ed. *The Baptist Encyclopaedia: A Dictionary of the Doctrines, Ordinances, Usages, Confessions of Faith, Sufferings, Labors, and Successes, and of the General History of the Baptist Denomination in All Lands, with Numerous Biographical Sketches of Distinguished American and Foreign Baptist, and a Supplement.* Philadelphia, Louis H. Everts, 1881; reprint, Paris, AR: Baptist Standard Bearer, 1988. S.v. "Carson, Alex., LL.D."

BY JOHN FRANKLIN JONES
CORDOVA, TENNESSEE
JULY 2004

THE BAPTIST STANDARD BEARER, INC.

a non-profit, tax-exempt corporation
committed to the Publication & Preservation
of the Baptist Heritage.

CURRENT TITLES AVAILABLE IN
THE BAPTIST *DISTINCTIVES* SERIES

KIFFIN, WILLIAM — A Sober Discourse of Right to Church-Communion. Wherein is proved by Scripture, the Example of the Primitive Times, and the Practice of All that have Professed the Christian Religion: That no Unbaptized person may be Regularly admitted to the Lord's Supper. (London: George Larkin, 1681).

KINGHORN, JOSEPH — Baptism, A Term of Communion. (Norwich: Bacon, Kinnebrook, and Co., 1816)

KINGHORN, JOSEPH — A Defense of "Baptism, A Term of Communion". In Answer To Robert Hall's Reply. (Norwich: Wilkin and Youngman, 1820).

GILL, JOHN — Gospel Baptism. A Collection of Sermons, Tracts, etc., on Scriptural Authority, the Nature of the New Testament Church and the Ordinance of Baptism by John Gill. (Paris, AR: The Baptist Standard Bearer, Inc., 2006).

CARSON, ALEXANDER	Ecclesiastical Polity of the New Testament. (Dublin: William Carson, 1856).
BOOTH, ABRAHAM	A Defense of the Baptists. A Declaration and Vindication of Three Historically Distinctive Baptist Principles. Compiled and Set Forth in the Republication of Three Books. Revised edition. (Paris, AR: The Baptist Standard Bearer, Inc., 2006).
BOOTH, ABRAHAM	Paedobaptism Examined on the Principles, Concessions, and Reasonings of the Most Learned Paedobaptists. With Replies to the Arguments and Objections of Dr. Williams and Mr. Peter Edwards. 3 volumes. (London: Ebenezer Palmer, 1829).
CARROLL, B. H.	*Ecclesia* - The Church. With an Appendix. (Louisville: Baptist Book Concern, 1903).
CHRISTIAN, JOHN T.	Immersion, The Act of Christian Baptism. (Louisville: Baptist Book Concern, 1891).
FROST, J. M.	Pedobaptism: Is It From Heaven Or Of Men? (Philadelphia: American Baptist Publication Society, 1875).
FULLER, RICHARD	Baptism, and the Terms of Communion; An Argument. (Charleston, SC: Southern Baptist Publication Society, 1854).
GRAVES, J. R.	Tri-Lemma: or, Death By Three Horns. The Presbyterian General Assembly Not Able To Decide This Question: "Is Baptism In The Romish Church Valid?" 1st Edition.

	(Nashville: Southwestern Publishing House, 1861).
MELL, P.H.	Baptism In Its Mode and Subjects. (Charleston, SC: Southern Baptist Publications Society, 1853).
JETER, JEREMIAH B.	Baptist Principles Reset. Consisting of Articles on Distinctive Baptist Principles by Various Authors. With an Appendix. (Richmond: The Religious Herald Co., 1902).
PENDLETON, J.M.	Distinctive Principles of Baptists. (Philadelphia: American Baptist Publication Society, 1882).
THOMAS, JESSE B.	The Church and the Kingdom. A New Testament Study. (Louisville: Baptist Book Concern, 1914).
WALLER, JOHN L.	Open Communion Shown to be Unscriptural & Deleterious. With an introductory essay by Dr. D. R. Campbell and an Appendix. (Louisville: Baptist Book Concern, 1859).

For a complete list of current authors/titles, visit our internet site at:
www.standardbearer.org
or write us at:

he Baptist Standard Bearer, Inc.
NUMBER ONE IRON OAKS DRIVE • PARIS, ARKANSAS 72855
TEL # 479-963-3831   *FAX # 479-963-8083*
EMAIL: Baptist@centurytel.net   *http://www.standardbearer.org*

Thou hast given a standard to them that fear thee; that it may be displayed because of the truth. — Psalm 60:4